Selling
Donald Dump

**A Public Service Initiative of the
Donald Trump De-activation Society**

by John F. Ince
a.k.a. The Rogue Writer

Published by:

The Serendipity Publishing Group

Email: info@serendigity.com

© John F. Ince, 2016

All Rights Reserved

ISBN-13: 978-1519635877

ISBN-10: 1519635877

Cover Caricature of Donald Trump Courtesy of the amazing

DonkeyHotey - See All His Work on Flickr here …

https://www.flickr.com/photos/donkeyhotey/

To order additional copies of this book visit:

www.Donald-Dump.com

Visit Donald Dump on Facebook at:

facebook.com/DonaldTrumpDeactivationSociety

John Ince's Twitter Handel: @johnince

For additional information or

for discounts on bulk orders email:

Info@Serendigity.com

We welcome comments and creative submissions

Email: donald@donald-dump.com

What They're Saying About *Selling*

Donald Dump

• It's brutal. It has more bite than a $10 million ad buy. – Barack O'Drama

• It not only gets inside the head of The Donald. It also gives a pitch perfect impersonation of the crazies who support him. - Anderson Scooper

• *Donald Dump* fights fire with fire. It's the force agains the farce. Or is it the farce against the force? Either way it's a farcical force that captures all the vulgarity and BS that characterizes Donald Trump's so called "campaign." – Billary Clintstone

• Frankly, I didn't find it very useful or amusing. - Sean Vanity, Foxy News

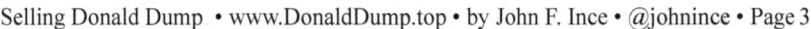

• There are three things I didn't like about this book. The font was too small. It was too long … and … and … I can't remember the third thing. Oops. - P. Rick Perry

• Even though the Donald and I both play the same crowd, I gotta say I cringed when I read this book. It was eerily on target.
- Rush Bimbo

• *Donald Dump* is high energy political parody. It puts the Donald in his place. There he is – lying in the gutter of politics." - Jeb Boosh

• Tucked away in Part 3 of this book is a brilliantly conceived strategy to take down the Donald. Where should I send the check? - David H. Kock

• This book stunk. Definitely won't make it into my library - but not many books do. - Ann Coolter

• *Donald Dump* captures the puffery, the platitudes and the political pollution that emanates from Donald Trump's oversized ego. - Al Bore

• Destined to become a classic of political parody. - *The New York Mimes*

• Spot on! If Mark Twain were alive today this is the kind of book he would write. - Mark's Twin

• It captures the shrill tones and cluelessness of the people are who supporting Donald Trump. Do they even realize they're getting Trumped by the Donald? - Dan Blather

• I hope all the Donald's supporters read this book and take a good long look at themselves in the mirror.
- Chris Chrispie Creme

• It exposes the Donald's pubescent personality. - Run Paul

• It brings into full view the pathological lies of Donald Trump.
- Burnie Sanders

• *G*ood old fashioned straight talk - red meat for both liberals and conservatives who fear the Donald.
- John McPain

• I've been taking shots at politicians for over 20 years and this book hits a very big target right between the eyes.
- John Skewart

• It's the most intelligent and insightful book out on Repugnicant politics today.
- Nancy Peloski

• Todd and I are indignified that we have been implied in this parodical publishment. - Saint Sarah Palin

• It's libelous! My lawyers are taking a serious look at this thing for ~~hysterical~~ historical inaccuracies. I'm going to sue this loser for everything he's got, which probably isn't much. He'll be hearing from my lawyers very soon. You don't mess around with the Donald or his lawyers. - Donald Rump

Table of Contents

Part 2 - Donald Trump Reality Warp - Page 29

Part 3 - Actual Reality - Page 75

Carnival Barker at the Traveling Circus?

Donald Dump is the personification of the craziness that has infected and infested the modern politics - where entertainment Trumps discourse - where insults Trump intelligence - where being terrific Trumps being thoughtful – where the Donald's ego runs wild and free.

Donald Dump is based on a real life character who in many ways is stranger than fiction. Who, in their right mind, could have made up *The Donald*, if he wasn't real? Is Donald Trump for real or is Donald Dump the real reality? It's difficult to know the difference when clowns are running the show? Perhaps it's all an infinitely reflecting set of mirrors – parody of parody of parody. The real Donald Trump is a blend of fact and fiction - a mixture of truth and falsehood - just like most of his fanciful claims about himself and his record.

In *Trump World*, politics has become a traveling circus. So we might as well send in the clowns. *Donald Dump* is more than a clownish caricature. Donald Dump is a movement and a marketing phenomenon. [1] We're promoting the Donald Dump brand as absurd abstraction. The Donald Dump brand is a non-sensical mirror image of the Donald Trump brand. It's a way for reasonable people, like us, to take steps to deal with the clowns who've have taken over the circus of politics. In sum, Donald Dump is the anti-dote to Donald Trump. Our goal is to push back against Donald Dump Reality Warp. To learn how we're going to do this … please check out part 3 of this book for our 3D plan to *De-Activate the Donald* [2] by literally puncturing his ballon sized ego.

---

[1] See page 31 - A (Bowel) Movement Begins ...

[2] facebook.com/DonaldTrumpDeactivationSociety

Send in the Clown [3]

Isn't he rich? What beautiful hair?
While we're on the ground, he's in mid-air.
Where is the clown?

Isn't he bliss? Does he approve?
He who keeps tearing around. Why can't we move?
Where is the clown? He must be the clown.

Just when he stops bashing the bores,
The crowd stands up and roars.
Making his entrance with his usual flair
Sure of his lines, but no one is there.

Don't you love farce? Don't you love hair?
I think that he wants what I want. Grab me a beer.
But where is the clown? Send in the clown.
The Donald is here.

Isn't he rich? What beautiful hair?
Why is he running so late in his career?
But where is the clown? He must to be the clown.
God help us - he's here.

---

[3] Adapted from Lyrics of song, *Send in the Clowns* popularized by Judy Collins

The Force Against the Farce

Looking as this circus through 3D glasses, we are *Donald Dump De-Activators* – invoking the binding, metaphysical force within ourselves to rid the political universe of the human farce called Donald Trump. Come along with us to the far out galaxy of modern politics to join the force against the farce. In business terms, Donald Trump has been packaging himself as a brand called, *The Donald.* We're now fighting fire with fire, by marketing the anti-Trump brand: Donald Dump. Donald Dump is the super-inflated ego of Donald Trump. Actually we didn't have put much air in it to make it a full blown caricature. Donald Trump had already blown it up to gigantic proportions. Donald Dump is that guy sitting in the Oval Office with a shit eating grin on his face and no clue what to do with 11 million immigrants – no clue how to work with Congress – or balance the budget – or deal with a crisis in the Middle East – or restore confidence after a financial meltdown – or regulate the Internet – or de-fuse the racial crisis – or stem the tide of violence in our schools – or do anything else that an experienced, tested, honest, fair and competent President would do.

Donald Dump is not just an alter ego. He's more than that - bigger than that - he's more terrific - more handsome and richer in the potential to ridicule. Donald Dump is everything that Donald Trump says *The Donald* is - even though he's not. *What pile of shit?* [4] The goal of the Donald Trump De-Activation Society to force that gigantic ego to go poop in the night. We have a seen a vision of Donald Trump's balloon sized ego punctured and transformed into nothingness. It's all very simple: Donald Dump uses the needle of ridicule to puncture the Donald's balloon. It's the perfect antidote to the Donald Trump phenomenon. *It's the force against the farce.*

---

[4] Donald Dump portrait by street artist, Banksy

Three Competing Realities

To greatly oversimplify the monumental challenge facing us, three alternative realities are actively competing for our attention in the modern world:
1) Media induced reality,
2) Donald Trump *Reality Warp*,
3) Actual reality.

Donald Trump has based his entire campaign on the supposition that a electorally sufficient number of Americans can't tell the difference between these three realities. This book brings the distinctions between them into clear focus using a handy, visual and navigational aid.

1. In Part 1 of this book we include a few choice snapshots of the world from the perspective of some of our powerful media outlets. YOU KNOW YOUR IN MEDIA INDUCED REALITY BECAUSE THESE ARTICLES ARE IN THIS FONT.

2. Part 2 of this book is the world seen as Trump Reality Warp. It's the only view Trump crazies are capable of seeing. This part might be amusing if it wasn't so real. Donald Trump's Reality Warp is set out in this font. It's called American Typewriter and it's the font screenwriters use when submitting a script to Hollywood movie moguls. Why? Well, because in many ways the Donald's campaign has to be a movie plot. Right?

3. Part 3 is actual reality … no avoidance here. **If you take nothing else away from this book, take the notion that we need to deal with the first two realities before we can deal with the last one.** In other words, we need *a Donald plan* and you'll find it too - in Part 3.

Part I

Media Induced
Reality

Ignoring Donald Trump didn't work for Republicans. What now? [5]

So now Republicans know that hoping it will all go away is not a successful strategy against Donald Trump. That raises a tough question: What, if anything, will work? The difference between the party's — and its presidential field's — more tentative approach to earlier Trump insults and the near-universal outrage that greeted his demand that all Muslims be barred from entering the country seemed to rest on a sense that Trump has maneuvered from politically disadvantageous territory to a place freighted with danger, whether for the Muslims he is characterizing as threatening or to the United States' strategic imperatives abroad. Like most of Trump's policy declarations, there was little to explain how he would do it, what the ramifications would be and how exactly it comported with the mores of a nation formed on religious freedom.

That aside, his latest bout of rhetorical exuberance left leading Republicans aghast and many of the party's presidential candidates in a squeeze. They have ignored or halfheartedly waved off insults uttered by Trump since the beginning of his campaign, against such key voter groups as Latinos and women. Even as his past remarks posed the potential of a mammoth problem for the party in 2016, many candidates were disinclined to confront him in any meaningful and persistent way.

Despite Trump's blatant insults, they also promised to support him should he win the nomination. Jeb Bush, the former Florida governor and possessor of a political lineage that has boomeranged against him this election season, is an example. He bumbled his response to Trump's insults toward Latinos — in one debate, he demanded that Trump apologize to Bush's Mexican-born wife but backed away when Trump refused. This week, he declared Trump was "unhinged." But Bush is still on the record as supporting Trump should the unhinged candidate become the nominee. This as Bush tries to convince Republican voters, in a new television ad, that he alone possesses the backbone to sit in the Oval Office. As Trump has ascended to the top of public opinion polls this year, he has been fueled by a hyper-charged, shock-driven media environment and his unique skills at salesmanship. But his tactics — us against them — have long been a staple of the nation's political landscape, particularly in times of economic stress and fear. And there has most often been a racial cant to the tactics.

---

5 http://www.latimes.com/politics/la-pol-ca-donald-trump-analysis-20151208-story.html

GOP PREPARING FOR CONTESTED CONVENTION [6]

By ROBERT COSTA AND TOM HAMBURGER, WASHINGTON POST

REPUBLICAN OFFICIALS AND LEADING FIGURES IN THE PARTY'S ESTABLISHMENT ARE PREPARING FOR THE POSSIBILITY OF A BROKERED CONVENTION AS BUSINESSMAN DONALD TRUMP CONTINUES TO SIT ATOP THE POLLS IN THE GOP PRESIDENTIAL RACE. MORE THAN 20 OF THEM CONVENED MONDAY NEAR THE CAPITOL FOR A DINNER HELD BY REPUBLICAN NATIONAL COMMITTEE CHAIRMAN REINCE PRIEBUS, AND THE PROSPECT OF TRUMP NEARING NEXT YEAR'S NOMINATING CONVENTION IN CLEVELAND WITH A SIGNIFICANT NUMBER OF DELEGATES DOMINATED THE DISCUSSION, ACCORDING TO FIVE PEOPLE FAMILIAR WITH THE MEETING. WEIGHING IN ON THAT SCENARIO AS PRIEBUS AND SENATE MAJORITY LEADER MITCH MCCONNELL (R-KY.) LISTENED, SEVERAL LONGTIME REPUBLICAN POWER BROKERS ARGUED THAT IF THE CONTROVERSIAL BILLIONAIRE STORMS THROUGH THE PRIMARIES, THE PARTY'S ESTABLISHMENT MUST LAY THE GROUNDWORK FOR A FLOOR FIGHT IN WHICH THE GOP'S MAINSTREAM WING COULD COALESCE AROUND AN ALTERNATIVE, THE PEOPLE SAID.

THE DEVELOPMENT REPRESENTS A MAJOR SHIFT FOR VETERAN REPUBLICAN STRATEGISTS, WHO UNTIL THIS MONTH HAD SPOKEN OF A BROKERED CONVENTION ONLY IN THE MOST HYPOTHETICAL TERMS — AND HAD TRIED TO ENCOURAGE A DRAMA-FREE NOMINATION BY LIMITING DEBATES AND SETTING AN EARLIER CONVENTION DATE. NOW, THOSE SAME LEADERS SEE A FLOOR FIGHT AS A REAL POSSIBILITY. AND SO DOES TRUMP, WHO SAID IN AN INTERVIEW LAST WEEK THAT HE, TOO, IS PREPARING. BECAUSE OF THE SENSITIVITY OF THE TOPIC — AND BECAUSE THEY ARE WARY OF SAYING SOMETHING THAT, IF LEAKED, WOULD PROVOKE TRUMP TO BOLT THE PARTY AND MOUNT AN INDEPENDENT BID — PRIEBUS AND MCCONNELL WERE MOSTLY QUIET DURING THE BACK-AND-FORTH. THEY DID NOT SIGNAL SUPPORT FOR AN OVERT ANTI-TRUMP EFFORT. BUT NEAR THE END, MCCONNELL AND PRIEBUS ACKNOWLEDGED TO THE GROUP THAT A DEADLOCKED CONVENTION IS SOMETHING THE PARTY SHOULD PREPARE FOR, BOTH INSTITUTIONALLY WITHIN THE RNC AND POLITICALLY AT ALL LEVELS IN THE COMING MONTHS. WHEN ASKED THURSDAY ABOUT THE DINNER AND CONVENTION PLANNING, SEAN SPICER, THE RNC'S CHIEF STRATEGIST AND SPOKESMAN, SAID: "THE RNC IS NEUTRAL IN THIS PROCESS, AND THE RULES ARE SET UNTIL THE CONVENTION BEGINS NEXT JULY. OUR GOAL IS TO ENSURE A SUCCESSFUL NOMINATION, AND THAT REQUIRES US THINKING THROUGH EVERY SCENARIO, INCLUDING A CONTESTED CONVENTION."

---

[6] https://www.washingtonpost.com/politics/gop-preparing-for-contested-convention/2015/12/10/d72574bc-9f73-11e5-8728-1af6af208198_story.html

WILL THE GOP MOUNT A THIRD-PARTY CHALLENGE TO TRUMP?

EXPERTS—AND HISTORY—SUGGEST IT'S AN INCREASINGLY PLAUSIBLE SCENARIO. AND COULD END IN DISASTER.

BY JEFF GREENFIELD, POLITICO 7

WITH DONALD TRUMP AS ITS STANDARD-BEARER, THE GOP WOULD SUDDENLY BE ASKED TO RALLY AROUND A CANDIDATE WHO HAS BEEN CALLED BY HIS ONCE AND FORMER PRIMARY FOES "A CANCER ON CONSERVATISM", "UNHINGED" "A DRUNK DRIVER...HELPING THE ENEMY." A PROMINENT CONSERVATIVE NATIONAL SECURITY EXPERT, MAX BOOT, HAS LABELED HIM FLATLY "A FASCIST." AND THE RHETORIC IS EVEN STRONGER IN PRIVATE CONVERSATIONS I'VE HAD RECENTLY WITH REPUBLICANS OF MODERATE AND CONSERVATIVE STRIPES. ... IF YOU WANT TO SEE THE MOST SULFUROUS ASSAULTS ON TRUMP, DON'T LOOK TO THE EDITORIAL PAGES OF THE NEW YORK TIMES OR THE COMMENTS OF MSNBC PERSONALITIES; LOOK INSTEAD TO THE MOST PROMINENT MEDIA VOICES IN THE CONSERVATIVE WORLD: NATIONAL REVIEW, THE WEEKLY STANDARD, COMMENTARY, AND THE COLUMNS OF GEORGE WILL AND OTHERS. IN PART, THEY DEPLORE HIS DEVIATIONS FROM THE CONSERVATIVE CANON; DEVIATIONS THAT FORMER REAGAN AIDE AND ONETIME FCC CHAIRMAN DENNIS PATRICK SUMMARIZES THIS WAY: "MANY OF MY COLLEAGUES FROM THE REAGAN ADMINISTRATION WOULD HAVE A HARD TIME PULLING THE LEVER FOR TRUMP. WE WEREN'T JUST REPUBLICANS, WE WERE CONSERVATIVES. IT IS VERY DIFFICULT TO SQUARE ANY PRINCIPLED THEORY OF CONSERVATIVE GOVERNANCE WITH MUCH OF WHAT TRUMP SAYS."

BUT IT'S MORE, MUCH MORE THAN POLICY THAT HAS STIRRED THE IRE ON THE RIGHT: IT'S THE VULGARITY, THE FUSION OF IGNORANCE AND ARROGANCE, THE NARCISSISM, THE DISSEMBLING ON MATTERS GREAT AND SMALL. THE COMPOSITE PORTRAIT OF TRUMP PAINTED BY THESE OUTLETS—LEAVENED ONLY BY A GRUDGING ACKNOWLEDGEMENT THAT HE'S TOUCHED ON LEGITIMATE CONCERNS ABOUT IMMIGRATION AND TERROR—MAKE THE IDEA OF HANDING OVER THE NUCLEAR CODES TO TRUMP UNSETTLING; AND IT MAKES THE IDEA OF EMBRACING HIM AS THE ALTERNATIVE TO CLINTON SOMEWHERE BETWEEN A REACH AND A LUNGE.
*** WHAT A TRUMP NOMINATION REPRESENTS, THEN, IS A VICTORY THAT LEAVES SIGNIFICANT SLICES OF THE PARTY UNWILLING OR UNABLE TO ACCEPT THE OUTCOME. WHETHER HE'S SEEN AS AN IDEOLOGICAL HERETIC FOR HIS VIEWS ON TRADE, TAXES, AND GOVERNMENT POWER, OR SEEN AS A DEMAGOGUE WHOSE CLOWNISH BLUSTER AND CASUAL BIGOTRY MAKE HIM TEMPERAMENTALLY UNFIT FOR OFFICE, THE ODDS ON MASSIVE DEFECTIONS ARE VERY HIGH.

---

7 http://www.politico.com/magazine/story/2015/12/donald-trump-2016-third-party-bid-213449

RUSH LIMBAUGH AND CONSERVATIVES REVOLT! [8]

THEIR HATRED FOR HOUSE BUDGET DEAL COULD HAND DONALD TRUMP NOMINATION

AMANDA MARCOTTE, SALON, DEC 18. 2015

IF YOU WANT TO TRULY UNDERSTAND WHY THERE'S A GOOD CHANCE THAT DONALD TRUMP COULD WIN THE REPUBLICAN NOMINATION, OVER THE (METAPHORICAL) DEAD BODIES OF MANY GOP ESTABLISHMENT TYPES THAT TRIED TO GET IN HIS WAY, LOOK NO FURTHER THAN THE RIGHT-WING MEDIA REACTION TO THE BUDGET AGREEMENT REACHED BETWEEN BY HOUSE REPUBLICANS. EVEN THOUGH REPUBLICANS GOT THEIR MOST IMPORTANT ITEM AGENDA ACCOMPLISHED — TAX BREAKS, AT THE EXPENSE OF INFLATING THAT DEFICIT THEY ONLY PRETEND TO CARE ABOUT — RIGHT-WING MEDIA IS ACTING LIKE A BUNCH OF QUISLING REPUBLICANS BOWED TO PRESIDENT BARACK OBAMA'S DEMANDS TO INSTITUTE SHARIA LAW WHILE PASSING SINGLE-PAYER HEALTH CARE.

REPUBLICANS CAVED ON A BUNCH OF RIGHT-WING NUT AGENDA ITEMS THAT THEY WERE NEVER GOING TO GET IN THE FIRST PLACE, ESPECIALLY THE DEMAND TO BAN MEDICAID PATIENTS FROM GOING TO PLANNED PARENTHOOD OR MAKING THE VISA PROCESS UNNECESSARILY LENGTHY FOR SYRIANS REFUGEES. NOR DID

THEY GO THROUGH THE POINTLESS GOVERNMENT SHUTDOWN DRAMA THAT HAS BECOME NEARLY ROUTINE UNDER THE OBAMA ADMINISTRATION. ... THE CONSERVATIVE BASE, WHICH IS SWIFTLY ABANDONING ANY PRETENSE OF IDEOLOGICAL MOTIVATION IN FAVOR OF SIMPLY IDENTIFYING AS THE ASSHOLE CONTINGENT, LOVES THESE SHUTDOWN DRAMAS, POSSIBLY MORE THAN THEY LOVE THE IDEA OF DEFUNDING PLANNED PARENTHOOD OR HOLDING SYRIAN FAMILIES IN REFUGEE CAMPS INDEFINITELY. THE IDEA OF BLACKMAILING THE PRESIDENT WITH THIS THREAT IN AN EFFORT TO BULLY HIM INTO SUBMISSION IS SO APPEALING THAT IT HARDLY MATTERS THAT IT DOESN'T WORK. BUT, AS IS INCREASINGLY TRUE ON A NUMBER OF FRONTS, THROWING RED MEAT TO THE CONSERVATIVE BASE MEANS ALIENATING THE ENTIRE REST OF THE COUNTRY, AND SO REPUBLICAN CONGRESSMEN, WHO PROBABLY JUST WANT TO GO HOME AND ENJOY CHRISTMAS WITH THEIR FAMILIES, TOOK A PASS THIS TIME. ... SO NOW THE RIGHT WING MEDIA IS EXPLODING IN RAGE.

---

[8] http://www.salon.com/2015/12/18
rush_limbaugh_and_conservatives_revolt_their_hatred_for_house_budget_deal_could_hand_donald_trump_
nomination/

Sean Hannity Praises Donald Trump's Tax Proposal As A "Serious Plan" [9]

Hannity: "I Like It A Lot"

SEAN HANNITY: I got to tell you, I like this plan. He's telling half of America, 75 million Americans, you will pay nothing in federal income taxes. And while many of them haven't been paying anyway, he's highlighting it. Smart move politically.

PETER JOHNSON, JR.: Devil's in the details, but he's also hijacking Democrat and independent voters. He's going straight into the heart of Democratic America and saying, listen, look at what Trump is doing. The billionaire wants to cut average Americans' taxes. I don't know whether he can do it or not. Maybe the numbers are there, maybe they're not. But it is a dramatic proposal that's going to change the emphasis of this election big time.

HANNITY: Charles, I agree with you. I think this is a serious plan for all the people that were critical, saying there's no substance. Charles Hurt, he is also saying a couple of other things need to happen. He needs to get rid of fraud, waste, and abuse, and he also said he would cut new deals with other entities, other countries. And I think what is the most underreported part of this is a one-time repatriation of corporate cash held overseas, a 10 percent one-time rate. We have trillions of dollars that corporations will not bring back to this country. Now with a lower corporate tax rate of 15 percent, that means businesses, America's open for business. We will be the tax safe haven that corporations and businessmen will go to if this becomes law. I like it a lot.
[...]

HANNITY: When you point out that 75 million Americans under this plan, Peter, will not pay a penny in federal income taxes, that is a huge plus. How does Hillary grab the narrative back that Republicans hate the poor?
JOHNSON: Very, very hard. And this goes to the heart of what we said week ago, that Donald Trump needs a policy. He needs a plan. He's coming up with a policy and a plan. The hard left likes to say that he's the George Wallace candidate of the 21st century. Now, with this plan that has meat on the bones, he's saying this is all about economic inequalty, economic inaction in this country. It's about take-home pay. How much are you taking home out of your check every week or every two weeks? And he says, I want to restore the American dream. I don't know if it can be done, but it's igniting a new paradigm of thought in this country.

HANNITY: I think it's going to advance a narrative. Now short of maybe a flat tax, a fair tax which conservatives want, this is a conservative plan.

---

9 http://mediamatters.org/video/2015/09/28/sean-hannity-praises-donald-trumps-tax-proposal/205835

Pastor Explains What Impressed Him About Donald Trump [10]

At the private meet-and-greet with dozens of pastors and religious leaders, GOP frontrunner Donald Trump addressed concerns that some in the African-American community have about perceived insensitivity to the plight of minorities.

Bishop George Bloomer, founder and pastor of the Bethel Family Worship Center, attended Monday's meeting, used the opportunity to ask Trump about his recent comments that a black lives matter activist "deserved to be roughed up" after heckling him at a recent campaign event.

"What impressed me was that I raised that question--I was the one who raised the question to talk to him about that--for a half hour to 45 minutes we discussed that issue," the Bishop said on Hannity.

"And how'd you feel after it," asked Sean.

"I felt good about that," the Bishop responded. "I was okay about what his answers to what we had put in front of him."

Also joining Sean was Dr. Mike Murdock, Pastor of the Wisdom Center. Murdock claimed that Trump sounded, "as real as any human could get" at Monday's meeting.
"He doesn't really have a filter, does he?" Sean said to Murdock.
"And that's the secret to his appeal," Murdock responded.
Bishop Wallace Cherry of the Compassion Worship Center was also impressed by Trump's sincerity.
"I just came with an open mind, to see what issues this man stands for," Cherry explained. "What he said today, I kind of felt that he was sincere, from the heart."
Watch Sean's interview with three ministers that attended Monday's private meet and greet with Donald Trump on Monday's Hannity.

---

[10] http://www.hannity.com/articles/election-493995/pastor-explains-what-impressed-him-about-14165269/

Donald Trump Really Doesn't Want Me to Tell You This, But ... [11]

BY MARK BOWDEN, Vanity Fair

I spent a long, awkward weekend with Donald Trump in November 1996, an experience I feel confident neither of us would like to repeat. He was like one of those characters in an 18th-century comedy meant to embody a particular flavor of human folly. Trump struck me as adolescent, hilariously ostentatious, arbitrary, unkind, profane, dishonest, loudly opinionated, and consistently wrong. He remains the most vain man I have ever met. And he was trying to make a good impression. Who could have predicted that those very traits, now on prominent daily display, would turn him into the leading G.O.P. candidate for president of the United States? ...

He has no coherent political philosophy, so comparisons with Fascist leaders miss the mark. He just reacts. Trump lives in a fantasy of perfection, with himself as its animating force. Before I met him back in 1996, I felt bad for him. He'd had a rough 10 years. He had just turned 50 and wasn't happy about it. He looked soft, from his growing jowls to the way his belt bit deeply into the spreading roll of his belly. As a businessman he had crashed and burned, rescued only by creditors who had to bail him out lest they be dragged down with him. His enterprises were being run by court-appointed managers, who had put him back on his financial feet mostly by investing heavily in Atlantic City, which was then on the rise.

He had insulated himself from failure with bluster. In public he was still The Donald—still rich, still working hard at being a symbol of excess ... It was hard to watch the way he treated those around him, issuing peremptory orders—"Polish this, Tony. Today." He met with the lady who selected his drapery for the Florida estate—"The best! The best! She's a genius!"—who had selected a sampling of fabrics for him to choose from, all different shades of gold. He left the choice to her, saying only, "I want it really rich. Rich, rich, elegant, incredible." Then, "Don't disappoint me." It was a pattern. Trump did not make decisions. He surrounded himself with "geniuses" and delegated. So long as you did not "disappoint" him—and it was never clear how to avoid doing so—you were gold. What was clear was how fast and far one could fall from favor. The trip from "genius" to "idiot" was a flash. The former pilots who flew his plane were geniuses, until they made one too many bumpy landings and became "fucking idiots." ...

TRUMP'S TURN TOWARD RACIALLY CHARGED FICTION CHALLENGES THE GOP [12]

LET'S NOT SUGARCOAT THINGS: DONALD TRUMP, THE REPUBLICAN FRONT-RUNNER FOR PRESIDENT OF THE UNITED STATES, IS SPREADING FALSEHOODS AND STOKING FEARS ABOUT BLACKS, MUSLIMS, AND LATINOS. THE DARK TURN IN THE RACE HAS CREATED SIGNIFICANT NEW CHALLENGES FOR HIS RIVALS — CHALLENGES MOST SEEM UNSURE HOW TO HANDLE. AFTER ALL, WHAT DOES ONE DO ABOUT A CANDIDATE WHO IS NECK-DEEP IN A FEVER SWAMP WHILE HEAD AND SHOULDERS ABOVE HIS RIVALS IN THE POLLS?

TRUMP HAS SURGED INTO A CLEAR LEAD AMONG REPUBLICANS IN SURVEYS SINCE THE DEADLY ATTACKS ON PARIS, AMID HEIGHTENED PUBLIC CONCERN OVER WHETHER AMERICANS FACE SIMILAR DANGERS AT HOME. IT'S A VEXING SITUATION FOR THE REPUBLICAN PARTY, WHICH HAS SPENT YEARS TRYING TO MOVE TOWARD A MORE WELCOMING TONE. TRUMP HAS SURGED INTO A CLEAR LEAD AMONG REPUBLICANS IN SURVEYS SINCE THE DEADLY ATTACKS ON PARIS, AMID HEIGHTENED PUBLIC CONCERN OVER WHETHER AMERICANS FACE SIMILAR DANGERS AT HOME. IT'S A VEXING SITUATION FOR THE REPUBLICAN PARTY, WHICH HAS SPENT YEARS STRUGGLING TO MOVE TOWARD A MORE WELCOMING TONE. HOW LONG CAN TRUMP GO ON DOMINATING THE RACE WITHOUT CAUSING LASTING DAMAGE TO THE BRAND, EVEN IF HE ULTIMATELY FAILS TO WIN THE NOMINATION?

THE LAST FEW DAYS HAVE BEEN DIZZYING. ...

TRUMP'S LATEST COMMENTS ARE NOT THE FIRST TIME HE HAS DELVED INTO UNSUPPORTED CONSPIRACY THEORIES AND OUT-OF-NOWHERE FACTS. THE WASHINGTON POST'S FACT CHECKER BLOG HAS AWARDED HIS STATEMENTS THE HARSHEST FALSE RATING OF ANY 2016 CANDIDATE. LIZ MAIR, A REPUBLICAN STRATEGIST LEADING A NEW OUTSIDE CAMPAIGN TO DERAIL TRUMP, TOLD MSNBC ... "HE LIKES KEEPING HIS BRAND QUITE APART FROM OTHER PEOPLE IN THE PARTY."

---

[12] http://www.msnbc.com/msnbc/donald-trump-racially-charged-fiction-challenges-gop?google_editors_picks=true

The GOP's Greatest Fears [13]

By Jim Newell Slate.com

The only thing more disastrous for Republicans than a convention floor fight is a Donald Trump nomination.

Happy Brokered Convention Day! No, no, there will not be any brokered major political party conventions …

"Republican officials and leading figures in the party's establishment," the Post reports, "are preparing for the possibility of a brokered convention as businessman Donald Trump continues to sit atop the polls in the GOP presidential race."

There hasn't been a floor fight over the GOP presidential nomination since 1976 or any undecided first-ballot votes for a nominee from either party since 1952. That's because there aren't really any "brokers" anymore, i.e., party officials who keep delegates in their pockets and horse-trade at the site. That's a very old-timey, machine-politics system that looks absolutely awful on television. Modern nominating conventions aren't intended to resolve nominating disputes in real time. Instead, they serve as a) well-choreographed PR events for each party to market itself as allegedly representative of the American people, and b) a way for the parties to pamper big donors and attend cheesy, depraved happy hours with evil lobbyists. Because a deadlocked convention, in which a party heads into a convention before a candidate has secured a majority of delegates, would be an unholy PR mess for a party—picture roughly 2,500 delegates, along with the candidates themselves, horse-trading on the floor as his or her own individual broker—the Republican Party will do everything in its power to avoid this outcome. If a top candidate is a wee bit short of a majority of delegates, the powers that be would try to nudge a few unbound delegates in the right direction to push the candidate over the top and avoid a scene.

The absolute worst nightmare for the party would be Trump as its presidential nominee. What makes a contested Republican convention slightly more possible this year than in previous cycles is that there is a fresh scenario that would constitute even worse PR for the party than a floor melee: Donald Trump winning the party's presidential nomination.

---

[13] http://www.slate.com/articles/news_and_politics/politics/2015/12/the_republican_party_fears_donald_trump_more_than_a_convention_floor_fight.html

How Donald Trump took the Republican Party by storm [14]

By STEPHEN COLLINSON, CNN

Donald Trump's political hurricane is no accident. It's been brewing in the Republican Party for decades. Yes, the wild force tearing through the Republican White House race is a reflection of the grass roots' current fury at government and a revolt against establishment party leaders that has already swept away the likes of former House Speaker John Boehner and his lieutenant, Eric Cantor. And it's at least partly an individual phenomenon based on the charismatic appeal of Trump himself. The billionaire's brash television virtuosity and mastery of social media has connected with an angry swath of Republican voters in a way no other candidate has managed and will be put to the test again ...

But the Trump tempest has long been building. GOP critics argue the party has brought his destabilizing intervention on itself by not squelching controversies like claims he helped fuel that President Barack Obama was not born in the United States or explosive rhetoric about illegal immigrants. This contentious atmosphere has detracted from the debate on the nature of authentic conservatism that many partisans had expected in the 2016 race....

The Republican Party's current trauma stretches back at least to the 1990s, if not earlier. It lies in a transformation that turned the GOP from a party of consensus government that produced presidents like Dwight Eisenhower and George H.W. Bush into a party of rebellion in which the rank and file are consumed with anger at party leaders who they believe habitually maneuver to block true conservatives from winning the nomination. ...

Add in two failed presidential campaigns by nominees John McCain and Mitt Romney -- whom many conservatives saw as dinosaurs of the Republican establishment -- an industry of political revolt fueled by social media and super PACS that enabled individuals to challenge party bosses, the echo chamber of right-wing talk radio and partisan television programing, and the stage was set for pent up grass-roots ire to erupt. "This election is about the essence of America," he said, looking directly into the camera. "(It's) about all of us who feel out of place in our own country, a government incredibly out of touch and millions with traditional values branded bigots and haters." "With Trump in the whole way, I cannot come up with a scenario where the Republicans can get through this," said Shea. "Either he bails and he takes his supporters with him. Or he stays and ruins the brand."

---

[14] http://www.cnn.com/2015/12/14/politics/donald-trump-republican-party-history/index.html

Ann Coulter On Paris Attacks: 'Donald Trump Was Elected President Tonight' [15]

Conservative commentator Ann Coulter took to Twitter Friday night to decry "Muslim immigration" and push Donald Trump's 2016 campaign in the hours after the STRING OF ATTACKS IN PARIS that left more than 127 dead.

Coulter, a Fox News contributor well known for her internet diatribes against MUSLIMS, JEWS, and Mexican IMMIGRANTS, said the tragedy all but ensured Americans would elect Trump the next President strong stance on immigration.

> **Ann Coulter**
> @AnnCoulter
>
> They can wait if they like until next November for the actual balloting, but Donald Trump was elected president tonight.
> 6:17 PM - 13 Nov 2015
> 3,170   5,018

> **Ann Coulter**
> @AnnCoulter
>
> Why does NO ONE say the obvious thing on TV?! It's insane. Don't want terrorism in US? Stop importing Muslims!
> 4:58 PM - 13 Nov 2015
> 5,654   7,549

---

15 http://talkingpointsmemo.com/livewire/ann-coulter-donald-trump-paris-tweets

Donald Trump's
Walmart Candidacy [16]

As a field of boutique candidates caters to the well-heeled, the frontrunner dominates the down-market demographic. Throughout the summer of Trump, then the autumn of Trump, and now into Trump-mas-tide, pundits and politicians alike have assumed that something would happen that would cause Trump's standing to deflate and his candidacy to go away. I'm not being superior about this: I assumed so, too.

But whatever that "something" will be, if it is to be, it did not happen in Las Vegas on Tuesday night. The debate ended as it began: Trump, dominant; the field of anti-Trumps, fragmented. If anything, the anti-Trump field seems even further from coalescing on Wednesday morning than it did before Tuesday night. What the debate did highlight, though, was that no single anti-Trump candidate has to date emerged as a party favorite. All of them have tied their careers to at least one policy radically unacceptable to much of the party.

Love Marco Rubio's eloquence, his inspiring life story, and his youthful personability? Last night, Rubio also confirmed that his top priority as president will be to lead the country into a much wider war in Syria.

Agree with Ted Cruz's ideological hard-line, relish his confrontations with congressional party poo-bahs? Last night showed that he's generally a slippery person, and that his real views on issues like immigration align as closely to the donor elite as do those of anybody else on the debate stage.
Glad to see the charismatic Chris Christie return to the big stage? ... But even when he stands tough, he's not standing tough for you ... he's so preoccupied with his fight against the bully Trump that he can never connect what matters to him to what matters to the people whose votes he wants. And so on through the roster: Kasich, Fiorina, Paul.

They're so horrified by Trump that they won't try to understand the concerns of his supporters, much less address those concerns in any effective way. Which leaves the Republican race looking like American retailing: many specialized stores to serve the various wants and wishes of the well-heeled—and one vast Trump super-store dominating the down-market all by itself.

---

[16] http://www.theatlantic.com/politics/archive/2015/12/donald-trumps-walmart-candidacy/420723/

'I Trolled Trump at a Frank Luntz Focus Group' [17]

A former Romney staffer lied his way into a Trump voter focus group to see for himself who was actually behind the mogul's rise in the polls—and maybe to have a little fun mocking them. He left terrified and sure that the GOP would again fail to take the White House. For Michael Wille, a former Mitt Romney campaign staffer, the opportunity came when he saw an ad on Facebook to get involved with a Donald Trump focus group led by Republican pollster Frank Luntz. Wille lied and listed his first choice for the Republican nomination as Trump, out of a morbid curiosity and a desire to be mischievous. And hey, they were willing to pay him a hundred bucks for his time.

"I was there supporting Trump, but trolling everyone at the same time," Wille said. "I needed to see for sure exactly what the people of our party were thinking about Trump. Now I'm totally convinced there is no way we're going to win the presidential race... [Trump supporters] are delusional... they're so pissed off at the establishment they want to send a message no matter what." ... He spent much of the next few hours denouncing Trump's ideas and challenging the other Trump supporters in the focus group. He argued against the Muslim ban, citing the creation of America on a desire to flee religious persecution; he defended the disabled reporter that Trump made fun of; and pushed back against the claim that "thousands" of Muslims cheered after the 9/11 attacks. ...

"He was agitating the group the entire time. You had 28 people who felt one way, but he felt completely different because his motives were different. Every time he would speak the whole group would erupt against him," Luntz told The Daily Beast. "It's annoying, but he actually belongs. There are people who vote tactically for political candidates as a way to send a message or to do damage... He represented a point of view of some Americans." In a strange way, Wille said, he now wants Trump to win the nomination. But only so that the businessman can lose by a landslide in the general election, and make an enduring point to the members of the Republican Party. "We're definitely going to lose. The party is going to fracture—these guys are so committed to Trump, they are going to defend him no matter what," said Michael Wille. "I want him to get the nomination to get completely destroyed in the general. The older generation in my party needs to understand we can't have this pro-war, anti-immigrant nonsense anymore... we need to lose this [election] in order to ever win again," Wille said. "He needs to get destroyed in order for us to understand the path forward.

---

[17] http://www.thedailybeast.com/articles/2015/12/13/i-trolled-the-trump-focus-group.html

Trump's Medical Report Is More Insane Than His Campaign, Somehow [18]

Donald Trump's doctor released a medical report so silly that when we asked the American Medical Association about its language, their spokesman started to laugh. Donald Trump's doctor appears to be just as bombastic as he is. It's the only conclusion to be drawn from a HILARIOUSLY BIZARRE LETTER that the mogul's doctor—Harold Bornstein—wrote about his yuuuugely terrific health. And the letter raises as many questions as it answers. Bornstein, a Manhattan gastroenterologist who shared a medical practice with his father, writes he has been Trump's doctor since 1980. His father, Jacob Bornstein, died in 2010 at the age of 93. But that didn't stop Trump from Twitter-thanking Bornstein the elder for writing up his letter. "I am proud to share this health report, written by the highly respected Dr. Jacob Bornstein of Lenox Hill Hospital," the mogul tweeted, linking to the letter. Trump later deleted the tweet, probably because Jacob Bornstein is dead.

Harold Bornstein, however, is very much alive and says Donald Trump is the picture of health. In the letter, he describes his health over the past few decades using language that veers from standard to bizarre. For example, he describes Trump's recent physical exam as "show[ing] only positive results." While it's clear he means to say everything was normal, the word "positive" is an odd use of the term in medicine. Rather, it typically means that some result or finding was present—and those findings aren't always great news (think testing positive for a disease). The wording is clearly chosen more for rhetorical effect than clear medical communication—and that choice left some experts scratching their heads.

Bornstein also describes Trump's "laboratory test results" as "astonishingly excellent" (without noting which tests were run). That is a weird thing to say, as not many doctors would describe themselves as "astonished" at their patient's lab results. Like Trump, Bornstein seems allergic to detail. ...

And then it goes completely off the rails. "If elected," Bornstein writes, "Mr. Trump, I can state unequivocally, will be the healthiest individual ever elected to the presidency."

---

[18] http://www.thedailybeast.com/articles/2015/12/14/the-donald-s-trumped-up-medical-report.html

MEDIA BURIED IN DENIAL ABOUT TRUMP [19]

... THE TIMES TWICE LAST WEEK STRESSED THAT GOP VOTERS MIGHT TURN AWAY FROM TRUMP IN FAVOR OF "MORE SOBER-MINDED CANDIDATES"; THAT THEY'LL TAKE "A MORE SOBER MEASURE OF WHO IS PREPARED TO SERVE AS COMMANDER IN CHIEF." SOBER-MINDED CANDIDATES? HAVE THESE PEOPLE BEEN WATCHING THE SPECTACLE THAT IS THE REPUBLICAN CAMPAIGN SEASON FOR THE LAST SIX MONTHS? THERE WAS NO BACKLASH -- QUITE THE OPPOSITE. TRUMP AND HIS XENOPHOBIC CAMPAIGN CONTINUE TO SOAR IN THE GOP POLLS AS HE UNFURLS AN ENDLESS STREAM OF OUTRAGEOUS PROPOSALS. (BRING BACK U.S.-SANCTIONED TORTURE! THE GOVERNMENT NEEDS TO CLOSE DOWN SOME AMERICAN MOSQUES!)

FACT: TRUMP REALLY HAS EMERGED AS THE PERFECT FOX NEWS ERA CANDIDATE. HE'S A BIGOTED NATIVIST. AND HE'S A BULLYING, CONGENITAL LIAR WHO WALLOWS IN MISINFORMATION. IN THE PROCESS, HE'S WINNING OVER THE DEMAGOGUERY WING OF THE REPUBLICAN PARTY THAT'S BEEN FEASTING OFF FAR-RIGHT MEDIA HATE RHETORIC FOR YEARS.

NOW, BY SUCCESSFULLY NEUTRALIZING ENOUGH MEMBERS OF THE PRESS, TRUMP'S CREATED SPACE FOR HIMSELF TO MANEUVER WHILE ESPOUSING JAW-DROPPING RHETORIC THAT IN THE PAST WOULD HAVE BEEN CONSIDERED DISQUALIFYING FOR ANY CANDIDATE. SO YES, OF COURSE TRUMP CAN WIN THE NOMINATION, PARTLY BECAUSE HE EMBODIES TODAY'S REPUBLICAN PARTY, AS REIMAGINED THROUGH THE INTOLERANT LENS OF FOX NEWS.

AFTER MONTHS AND MONTHS OF PREDICTING THE "BEGINNING OF THE END" OF TRUMP'S RUN, THE PRESS OUGHT TO FORTHRIGHTLY CONCEDE HE COULD REPRESENT THE GOP NEXT NOVEMBER, WHILE AT THE SAME TIME AGGRESSIVELY CHRONICLE THE UNPRECEDENTED EXTREMISM THAT'S PROPELLING HIS RUN.

INSTEAD, THE CAMPAIGN PRESS TODAY SEEMS POORLY EQUIPPED TO HANDLE WHAT'S HAPPENING TO THE REPUBLICAN PARTY, ... THAT SIGNATURE PRESS TIMIDITY SEEMS TO SPRING FROM A LARGER RELUCTANCE TO FACE THE REALITY OF TODAY'S GOP. DESPERATE TO KEEP ALIVE A LONG-OUTDATED, ASYMMETRICAL MODEL THAT SUGGESTS PARTISAN BATTLES IN WASHINGTON, D.C., ARE FOUGHT BETWEEN CENTER-LEFT DEMOCRATS AND CENTER-RIGHT REPUBLICANS, THE PRESS SIMPLY DOESN'T WANT TO ACKNOWLEDGE THE GOP'S RADICAL RIGHT TURN. BUT IT'S THAT DEFINING LURCH THAT'S OPENED THE DOOR FOR A POSSIBLE TRUMP WIN. MEANING, YOU CAN'T UNDERSTAND TRUMP'S SURGE WITHOUT UNDERSTANDING THAT THE GOP HAS DISMANTLED THE GUARDRAILS; THAT IT'S NOW ANYTHING GOES.

---

[19] http://mediamatters.org/blog/2015/11/23/beltway-media-still-buried-in-denial-about-trum/207029

My Morning Advice: Don't Talk About Taking Down Donald Trump. Just Take Him Down. [20]
—By Kevin Drum

Here's the latest on GOP panic over the possibility that Donald Trump might actually win the Republican nomination: A well-connected GOP operative is planning a "guerrilla campaign" backed by secret donors to "defeat and destroy" the celebrity businessman's candidacy, ... In the absence of our efforts, Trump is exceedingly unlikely to implode or be forced out of the race," according to the Trump Card memo. "The stark reality is that unless something dramatic and unconventional is done, Trump will be the Republican nominee and Hillary Clinton will become president."

....Ms. Mair, who has ties to the libertarian movement and the GOP establishment, said that donors backing Texas Sen. Ted Cruz, Mr. Kasich and Mr. Bush are interested, and that some worry that going public could hurt their candidate. Look, folks: the first rule of fight club is that you don't talk about fight club. What's the point of publicly announcing about this strategy? It's good for the ego, I suppose, but all it does is alert Trump and ruin any jolt of surprise you might get from your campaign. Now reporters are all ready for it, and when it happens they'll just dissect it dispassionately instead of (hopefully) being dazzled. It's like the idiots in the Hillary Clinton campaign who decided to alert the world that they planned a campaign to make Hillary look more human. Nice going.

As with most liberals, I'm of two minds about all this. On the one hand, Republicans deserve every bit of what they're getting. For years they've been actively encouraging the enraged, racially-charged grievance culture that Trump represents, and it's hard to feel sorry for them now that it's biting them in the ass. Besides, if Trump does win the nomination, he's almost certain to lose, and that's fine with me. Republicans deserve another few years out in the cold. On the other hand, life is strange, and "almost certain" is not "certain" What's more, we're now at the point where Trump is no longer a joke. Another year of his unapologetic racism and xenophobia could do serious damage to the country—and especially to the targets of his malignant rants. It's long past time to dump him on the nearest ash heap of history.

---

[20] http://www.motherjones.com/kevin-drum/2015/11/my-morning-advice-dont-talk-about-taking-down-donald-trump-just-take-him-down

Part II

Donald Trump
Reality Warp

Is he a Demigod or a Demagogue?

When the Donald first announced, it seemed like a joke. Three months later, it was no laughing matter when he was still leading in the polls. *This is crazy!* I was thinking when I ran into an old friend who also had the Donald on the brain, "He terrifies me," she says. "He a demagogue. I'm a student of history. This is how other demagogues rose to power. This is what happened in Nazi Germany during Hitler's rise. People are embracing this guy and he's very dangerous. What worries me most is what is says about the American electorate. *Who are these crazies?"*

"Don't worry," I say, "At this point in the campaign the polls means nothing." Four years ago, a whole host of imposters led in he polls, then – they all faded … Don't worry."

"I hope you're right." She says.

No, I was wrong. The Donald hasn't faded. He's still levitating and has plenty of money to sustain the illusion. On December 28, 2015 Newsweek ran the headline: DONALD TRUMP TIES WITH POPE FRANCIS IN POLL FOR SECOND MOST ADMIRED MAN IN WORLD. [21] Now, I'm really worried - so worried that I've decided to do something. What you're reading now is the result. This is caricature – not only of the Donald but it's also a parody of the crazies who are supporting him. That's what's so terrifying about all this. Just who are these people that you see on television at The Donald's rallies? Who are these crazies? To get some insight into this great mystery of our time, read on about the Donald Trump Reality Warp …

---

[21] http://www.newsweek.com/donald-trump-ties-pope-francis-poll-409277

A (Bowel) Movement Begins
by Josiah Frumpacker

The Donald Dump Bowel Movement all started one day when I was having breakfast at the Squat and Gobble in Queer Creek, just up the road from the Blubber House Bar. I reached across the tray to butter my toast, when I se-ed what appeared to be something that stood out in this pat of butter - The Donald's face. "It's a sign." I thought to myself. The Donald's likeness has been implanted unto the pat of butter. Until then it had only been a name. But now it was more than that. It was a prophesy of what was to come." That's the first time I started to see the image of the Donald's likeness everywhere.

I decide to make a bold move. It was risky because, remember, "Not everyone knew about The Donald back then. He wasn't the household brand that he is now. He wasn't the larger than life ego that he is today. His marketing juggernaut and political aura was barely more than a forethought back then.

At that point in time, I was only Charter Member of the Donald Trump Admiration Society." The Donald's memoir - The Art of the Steal." had not yet even been ghostwritten. So back then it was not easy, being the first and only member.

Skeptics scoffed at me. Our organization didn't have big time media support and but we did have the Donald - and as it turns out that was enough. IN FACT - it was plenty to launch was has now become the most terrific thing to happen to American politics in eons. - Josiah Frumpacker

Donald Dump's Staff Directory

Josiah Frumpacker - Founder: Editor in Chief. Former hot air balloonist from the Hamptons and part time bartender at Luigis in Freeport, Long Island. Great sense of vision & a very dry wit.

Anita Mandalay - Official Greeter: Former waitress at The Big Beaver Lick, in Queens, New York. A sweetie once you really get to know her, as Donald has done many times.

Lily Farnquist: Spelling Specialist. Stature belies her quaint demeanor. 5' 2" of sheer might. No holds barred.

Hazle Nutt - Volunteer Coordinator: One Wacky Woman - Moments of civility wrapped in a package of total insanity.

Lois Price - Official Shopper: Bargain hunter supreme. Hired as consultant after Ivanna 's ill-considered shopping spree.

Art Clogfaart DTDS - Museum Curator: Old chum of Donald Dump's at the Wharton School. Part time hairdresser.

Suzy Squeamish - Specialist: Tireless dancer. Formerly with the Blubberhouse Bar in Quogue, New York.

Dick Hunter - Chief Recruiter: Always on the lookout for new and exciting talent to beef up Donald Dump's Team.

Dr. Gass - Official Anesthesiologist: Laugh a minute on site physician - Always ready with a gag.

Evan Keel - Policy Analyst: Thoughtful and well considered position papers that always see two sides to every issue.

Harry Rump - Official Plumber: Expert at fixing leaks in Donald Dump's ass, which happens more than he'd like to admit.

It's Going To Be Terrific

Documenting History: The first thing we realized was that we needed to get everything down on paper ... and everything needed to be **"terrific."** This was a challenge because, not many of us who have been editorializing this book are good with words - so some of this book may seem to be not so well written. Also, we were in a race with time to get this seminole work to the publisher (ie us) so that it might be made available to the pubic for sale before the Donald confligrates on the national political stage.

Speed Writing: Some of us in the editorial war room, had to take a crash course in speed writing and may not yet have mastered the craft of wordage - resulting in less than optimal word usage, errant grammar, unwise punctuation, and slightly daft spelling. This was entirely beyond our control. Given the time constraints we faced in finishing the book to completion in time for timely publication, we had to take some calculated risks word wise - just like the Donald has done throughout his extinguished career.

Our Apologies: If this unintentionally has resulted in your difficulty in the reading or understanding of our words and their meaning, then we offer our sincerest apologies in advance for any inconvenience it has or will cause to our readers and the broader audience for our book – including you and yours.

Timing: This book is very timely, as it's timed to be coincident with the Donald's Presidential ambitious. Is that just a coincidence time wise? We wonder sometimes about that. Does it make you wonder too? What we really believe in the depth of our collective psyche is that Donald Dump was channeling all that you are now reading through our minds to you the reader in it's present form. This, if true, is worthy of your awe and wonder.

- Sincerely, The Editorial Staffs

Exclusive:

Donald Trump Interviews Donald Dump

Donald Trump: How do you feel about people referring to you as "The Donald?"

Donald Dump: I like it. It's a term of respect. People recognize that because I've been enormously successful in business ... and by the way my financial statements show that I'm worth well over $7 billion ... that I'm due more respect than others in our society who aren't as smart, good looking and successful as I am.

Donald Trump: Kind of like putting yourself up on a pedestal.

Donald Dump: Exactly, and I deserve to be on a pedestal. I'm thinking of having Donald Dump Pedestals installed at the entrances to all Federal buildings when I'm elected. It will be a bust of me combing my hair back with a wave to the masses. Nice touch – don't you think?

Donald Trump: Yes, terrific. We totally agree ... a very sweet and sincere gesture to all the little people who so look up to you as their master. And you can have "The Donald" inscribed in big bold letters for everyone to see and admire.

Donald Dump: I like that. I'll take it under consideration.

Donald Trump: So let's talk a little bit about your gigantic ego. Did you have to work on pumping it up or did that just come naturally.

Donald Dump: It came very naturally to me. When you're as successful as I am the ego grows with your net worth. Success is all about marketing and if you've got something as powerful as my persona to market ... hey, why hold back? Mae West was right, "If you've got it flaunt it."

Donald Trump: That you have done. Now let's move onto your thoughts about the other Repugnicant candidates for President. Are you satisfied with the current crop of candidates?

Donald Dump: Who could be satisfied? What a bunch of losers! If I wasn't running, this campaign season would have long since put everybody to sleep. I'm the only one who's waking people up.

Donald Trump: Is that why you threw your ego into the ring?

Donald Dump: It was more than that. I felt I had a personal responsibility to America to give myself to the people. Listen, I'm the Donald. I'm rich. I'm handsome. I'm the stuff of success. This is what America wants.

Donald Trump: So you're running just to buy America a little present?

Donald Dump: You can think of it like that - and it's even more. All the other candidates are basically whores. They sell themselves to their donors, But I don't have to prostitute myself. I already own myself. No soft peddling myself to the campaign contributors. I just buy myself. That's the beauty of my campaign. I already own the candidate.

Donald Trump: Amazing! Let's talk about some possible running mates. Some commentators are talking about a dream ticket - you and Sarah Palin? How 'bout that?

Donald Dump: Sarah Palin has a very classy chassis.... but she's a used car now. She has no resale value so let's just leave her on the lot.

Donald Trump: How about Snit Romney?

Donald Dump: Good looking contours ... square jaw ... good hair ... telegenic ... but there's nothing under the hood. Besides he's a proven loser.

Donald Trump: What about John Kasich?

Donald Dump: He's vintage Chevrolet with big fins .... but only appealing to a very small segment of the population ... a niche model.

Donald Trump: How about Jeb Bush?

Donald Dump: He's damaged goods. The Bush Brand is really banged up.

Donald Trump: So then how about Ted Cruisin'?

Donald Dump: He's a got a big base. I like that. The real issue with him is all that religious baggage he's got in the trunk. If we can find a way to toss off all that excess weight he might be the model I'm willing to drive. Too early to tell.

Donald Trump: Then of course there's P.Rick Perry?

Donald Dump: Yes, I liked him – for about 3 minutes. He's a Dodge pickup. Good if all you want to drive around the ranch and holler, "Yee haw!" Other wise, he's useless. He's gone back to his Texas pasture now.

Donald Trump: How about Crisp Crispie Creme?

Donald Dump: He's gas guzzler ... a big SUV who wouldn't take us anywhere.

Donald Trump: How about Carly Purina?

Donald Dump: That dog? She barks too much. I never take pets when I'm traveling.

Donald Trump: How about Marco Rubi-Uh-Oh?

Donald Dump: His name says it all - too much risk with a new model. He hasn't been road tested. Besides he's Latino. I'm not even sure he's got a birth certificate.

Donald Trump: How about Ben Person?

Donald Dump: You mean the Doctuh? He's a Mini ... consumes very little energy ... but you can't fit anything else inside cabin... I don't travel light you know.

Donald Trump: Okay ... let's move onto your possible Democrapic opponent. How about Colonel Sanders?

Donald Dump: Isn't he a scream? We haven't had the likes of him since Howard Dean. But, he has zero chance of getting the

nomination - a Democrapic Socialist in the White House? Come
on ...

Donald Trump: What about Lincoln Chaffee?

Donald Dump: Who?

Donald Trump: He's that the guy with no dentures from from
Vermont or Rhode Island or someplace like that ... you
remember him?

Donald Dump: I must have overslept that morning. I'll have to
check him out. What's his name
again?

Donald Trump: Chaffee ... So
that leaves us with Billary C?
What's your take on her?

Hairbrained

Donald Dump: Nice lady, but
again, she's got too much
baggage – so much, you can't fit
it all inside the trunk and the
chassis. You need to hire a u-
haul. Then there's that other guy sitting in the back seat talking
non stop. Nobody wants somebody like him in the car with you.
Besides, her engine keeps sputtering ... high maintenance
vehicle. Have you read about all the infighting in her campaign?
I'm not a mechanic. When I buy a car I want it to run smoothly.
Last time around, she drove her campaign right into a ditch. We
can expect the same this time around.

Donald Trump: So I guess that seals it - The Donald is a shoo
in.

Donald Dump: Exactly! Hey here's a little something for your
time - a Donald Dump branded tie - imported from China - wear it
proudly. When I'm elected all our ties will be made in U.S.A,
because I'm the Donald and anything the Donald says - goes.

The Gospel According to the Donald
In the Donald's Own Words

"Don't get me wrong. I like God. God has done a lot of good for a lot of people in the world and he's deserves every bit of credit he gets in churches. But God isn't the Donald - by any measure. God's numbers are way down. He'll get what maybe a hundred or so in church on Sunday but 70,000 fill the football stadium and millions more watch on TV. Frankly, God isn't all that exciting any more. He seems very low energy these days. God doesn't seem to have the pep that he used to have. Even people who still worship God, do it in mumbles. They congregate in secret and use all kinds of mumbo jumbo that frankly I don't think even they get. It's all parables and hocus pocus. Whereas me - I'm a straight shooter. I tell it like it is.

In terms getting things done, God has been falling down on the job. I don't think he really understands business or how to negotiate. His churches aren't doing that well. Frankly I think God is in way over his head. The world has gotten too complex for him. God doesn't have a clue about financial derivatives. I do. And God tries to take both sides of too many issues. He sends mixed signals to his supporters. They can't seem to decide whether he's for violence or against it. He has no policy in the Middle East. I don't think his staff has a clue what to do there. It's a real leadership vacuum. Even God's supporters are in disarray. They're on the defensive. God doesn't know how to play offense. If they pray at all, the usually do it in private. Or in if they do it in public, they get called out for it. Nobody in the media likes God these days. His poll numbers are way down. ... and my numbers are way up. There's a reason for this. God doesn't get the way marketing works today. He's still using 16th century techniques. You almost never see God on the evening news, but I'm there 24/7. God can't seem to figure out the social media. Frankly, I've got God beat hands down in media mentions. How many followers does God have on Twitter? See, you don't even know. But everybody knows my Twitter handle: @DonaldDump. That tells you something right there."

The Donald's Ten Commandments

The Almighty dollar is the Lord your God and hath brought you out of the house of bondage.

$ ONE: Thou shalt have no other gods besides The Donald.

$ TWO: Thou shalt make of The Donald a campaign image --the likeness of which is everything on television, or that is on the Internet, or that is in the media in any form.

$ THREE: Thou shalt not take the name of The Donald in vain.

$ FOUR: Thou shalt keep image of the Donald holy.

$ FIVE: Thou shalt not honor thy lobbyists and campaign contributors.

$ SIX: Thou shalt not admit immigrants from South of the border or the Middle East.

$ SEVEN: Thou shalt not commit political adultery.

$ EIGHT: Thou shalt not steal attention from the Donald.

$ NINE: Thou not shalt bear false witness against the Donald.

$TEN: Thou shalt not covet other candidates campaign contributions; for thou hath been blessed by thy Donald's personal real estate portfolio and the market value of the Donald's brand to be Lord of all.

Donald Dump's Bio

As Seen Through The Eyes of A Crazy

By Robert E. Lee Gibbons

Adjunct Professor of History at Trump University and
President of the At Large Chapter of the
Donald Dump Admiration Society

Précis: An analysis of the biographical underpinnings of Donald Dump's personality, history, biography, career and beliefs.

Introduction: Will historians one day look back and call Donald Dump the man of the hours. That's for time itself to decide? Yes, he has achieved a meteoric rise to fame and stardom? Yes his personage is worthy of history's highest accolades. But is that enough in today's world for an ego as big as his?

The Early Years: Donald Dump joined the race of humanity on a snowy laden mid Winters day in February 11, 1964 entering through his mother's womb at an undisclosed location in Queens, New York. After a brief youth, that has largely been glossed over by historians, he quickly became one of the most outstanding business executives and thought leaders in America. In 1977, when others were buying golf clubs he bought his first golf course, and was announcing to all the world that Trump Airlines flies.

The Making of a Master

Education: The Donald graduated himself by his bootstraps in 1964 from the New York Military Academy - and later from Fordham University and the Wharton School of high finagling. Upon graduation he quickly made a name for himself by buying New York real estates and airlines and plastering himself all over the doors and wings. Not long after, he made his mark on fashion and beauty industry by marrying Ivanna Trump who immediately became his wife. Partly because of his love of beauty he also bought the Miss America pageant, pledging to make America's women beautiful again.

Mr. Congeniality: But let's not get ahead of ourselves. The Donald was by now quickly establishing himself as "Mr. Congeniality" in New York City business and social circles. Although he owned resorts and gold golf courses galore, he was not content with lolly gagging on the links or the beach. Instead. he started working hard to make himself and the Donald Dump brand famous throughout business sectors and also on television.

Thrust Into the Spotlight: Towards that end, he accepted the role of Donald Trump on the reality TV show - The Appendix. The original version of that show did not go well. Viewers apparently were not interested in watching doctors remove patients appendices. Although the show was canceled after two episodes, The Donald was undeterred and after a spelling mistake on a memo, he got the idea to instead turn the show into an extended job interview and change the name to The Apprentice. The show as an instant hit and it catapulted The Donald into the stratosphere of television stardom, where he became an overnight sensation and instant celebrity in the tradition of Bob Barker and Hugh Downs.

A Political Dynamo Emerges

High Profile: Donald Dump's political beginnings began over his burgeoning views about public finance and of revenues that were flowing like waves in a sea crashing upon the shores of the economy. He was a military cadet too. The Donald became convinced by himself and his strong feelings about this. As a consequence, he became something of an outspoken spokesperson. With this as an auspicious beginning, he started making a higher profile for himself. His rise is even more impressive, considering that he was not yet a Presidential candidate. He was on an upward trajectory political wise now and did not complete ascent until he entered the ring as an erstwhile declared candidate for the Presidency in the fateful year of 2015. . Sagaciously, he registered with the Repugnicants and ran officially in this political affiliation of his party hence forth.

Presidential Ambitions: As now a President in Waiting, he prepared to serve two terms in office beginning in 2017 after his acceptance speech. Most of this time he was in preparation for what was to unfold as one of the most amazing political spectacles ever witnessed on the face of the earth before. He easily defeated all the other hopefuls in the first Repugnicant debate even though the questioning from Megan Kelly was over the top. Instead of complaining, he platformed on the issues of immigration, waste in spending and high taxes, and the fact that Carley Purina and Run Paul look funny. It touched a resonant nerve with the voters. Suddenly the Donald was connecting in a visceral way with the voters who were fed up with business as usual stalemating in Washington. Although he did not openly mention this, he evinced strong opposition to women having chosen abortion over others alternative means of abstinence including gun rights, and term limits and others campaign matters. By now the Donald's Presidential ambitions were in full swing and his election was looming on the horizon of life.

Political Career

Building the Brand: By now the Donald Dump legend was growing like weeds on a summer day. For example, in his office in the Dump Tower, kept a jar on his desk with the names of important personages he personally knew. Once a day, he plucked a name from it and dialed them on the telephone asking: "How's the Donald doing?" They all answered, "Great!" This was the secret to his brand and network building - personal connection - augmented by an insatiable thirst for knowledge.

Developing Connections: And the Donald is savvy with finances too. Using hard earned income inherited from his inheritance, he developed a plan to buy up everything that had low property taxes using municipal bonds, and other creative financing techniques he build a real estate portfolio second to none. He single handedly improved roads and sewers, and bolstered law and order in the Big Apple even though he wasn't officially elected to anything yet.

He developed close working relationships with Police Departments and others notables. He also personally built new bike paths on his golf course and storm-water treatment facilities, while raising a family, getting divorced twice, bankrupting four times and smiling like it was nothing at all. At the same time, he started planning for the Donald Dump Museum and started construction of a the Donal Dump Library near the 18 hole of his Westchester Country Club. He eventually plans to donate his book - The Art of the Steal to the library, but the terms of that deal are still being negotiated by his lawyers.

The Wall: During his second term as a successful businessman, the Donald introduced a ballot measure proposing the construction of a "National Wall" around the entire United States not including the oceans, as that might adversely impact the views of his condo tenants who have houses on the beach. His objective was to make America Great Again.

Innovative Tax Policies: The new wall was to be financed by a 0.5% sales tax increase. The $14.8 trillion facility was to be part of a multi-use shopping mall, and golf course which would extend along the entire perimeter of the Untied United States. It was projected to be built on time and under budget, but the federal government mucked things up and stalemated it despite the fact that millions thought it was a good investment of public money.

Digging Deeper: This failure of our leadership in Washington left a lasting impression on the Donald. He could see that the status quo in Washington just wasn't working as originally imagined by our founding fathers. During this period, which was admittedly tough to take for the future President, he looked into his own soul and dug deeper, until eventually mustering intestinal fortitude that has become the signature statement of his political campaign since then.

Donald the Evangelist: The Donald has had a tentative relationship with the conservative evangelical movement. They're not quite sure what to make of the Donald's religious views. To clear up any potential confusion the Donald recently released an official statement on God, which we may take as the Gospel According to the Donald.

Inside the Mind of the Real Donald
An Exclusive from WEGO Radio

WEGO Radio: Today, as our guest we have perhaps the biggest ego in the world today - Donald Dump. Please welcome "The Donald." (Sustained Applause)

The Donald: Okay, what's on your mind. I'm a busy guy.

WEGO Radio: With big egos all over the political spectrum, your ego stands tall above all the others. But of all your smart moves, the smartest was referring to yourself as the Donald. That was a stroke of genius and the ultimate statement about your ego. When did you start calling yourself "The Donald?"

The Donald: I was looking in the mirror one day ... which by the way is fun for a handsome guy like me to do - and we have mirrors everyplace in the Tower ... and I was admiring my hair. I thought to myself, Who's that good looking guy in the mirror? And I said to him, "The Donald, you're a winner." The Donald looked back at me - looked me right in the eye and said, "Well, you know what, The Donald, you're a winner too." It just came naturally. The Donald thing just suggested itself to both of us."

WEGO Radio: That's a true story, folks and you heard it first here on WEGO radio? And so that's how you and your ego bonded?

The Donald: Yes, it became a lasting bond and mutual statement of admiration between my ego and I. The Donald's ego and I just kind of agreed right then and there that we'd start referring to each other as "The Donald."

WEGO Radio: I'm sure big egos everywhere are inspired by stories like this of your rise from obscurity to ubiquity.

The Donald: Well they should be inspired. Because to refer to me as The Donald is really code for your belief in a terrific guy. It shows your good taste and by the way that's why my numbers are so good. People want to identify with a winner.

Fixed Trump's hair

WEGO Radio: Now, moving along, what part if any of having a big ego is honoring your word.

The Donald: It's everything. I mean when you've got ego like mine, people will believe anything you say. So what you say needs to be true. That's why I'm always true to my word.

WEGO Radio: So do you consider declaring bankruptcy and stiffing your creditors honoring your word?

The Donald: Wait, is this an ambush? Let's back up here. I have never declared personal bankruptcy. Never! The four bankruptcies you're referring to were my companies. They went bankrupt, not me. There's a big difference. Ask any lawyer. I do, and by the way, I've got the best legal team money can buy.

WEGO Radio: But didn't you own the companies that declared bankruptcy?

The Donald: Of course I did ... what don't I own? But owning a company isn't the same thing as being the company. When a company defaults and goes back on their legal and financial commitments, it's the company that's doing all that ... do you understand kid ... it's entirely different.

WEGO Radio: Wait ... you lost me there. Aren't the people like you who run the companies responsible for what the company does?

The Donald: Not at all. Ask any lawyer. A company is a legal fiction. The company is responsible for what it does. That's why we have companies ... and corporate charters written by smart lawyers so that the people who own and run them don't have to be personally on the hook if the company tanks. Do you know anything about business, kid?

WEGO Radio: What I know about business is that the guys at the top usually end up either exploiting or screwing the guys at the bottom, And ... being the big ego that you are, you're one of the guys at the top whose not only been screwing everybody else, but no you're running for President and trying to convince these people that you screwed that you're one of them?

The Donald: Listen I've been very nice to you – probably much nicer than I should have been. I didn't have to take time out from my campaign to be here. I thought this was a good opportunity for my ego shine. So ... is there a question?

WEGO Radio: Sure, why should anybody in their right mind vote for you?

The Donald: Well, first off let's be honest here. How many of the people out there are in their right mind? I mean they're working 9-5 sitting in a cubicle some place. They're bored out of their minds. When they get home they're so tired they don't have the energy to do anything but flip channels or surf the Web. Sooner or later they end up watching me on The Apprentice and they're immediately in a trance, because well, I'm a pretty good looking guy and very credible. They can't tell what's real and what's not real. All they know is that I'm familiar to them and I entertain them. So ... to answer your question ... people should vote for me because I'm a an amazing guy and I'm whole lot more entertaining than any other candidate out there.

WEGO Radio: So that's what politics is all about today - entertainment?

The Donald: Where have you been? It's been like that forever. Ronald Reagan was an entertainer pure and simple. We all look up to him today because he communicated so well. JFK beat Nixon because he was nicer to look at. Lincoln was a great storyteller. Joe Sixpack has no clue what any politician actually stands for. They vote for people because they like watching them. If they don't like to look at you they won't vote for you. And by the way I stand by what I said about Carly Purina or whatever that dog's name is.

WEGO Radio: Okay, you're being honest. I like that. Just how much of being a big ego is making the other guy feel small.

The Donald: It's really the key. When you shrink the other guy's ego, you make yourself seem much bigger. Egos are all relative. Make the other guy, who nobody liked anyway, feel small and everybody thinks you're a hero for it. Most of what I say isn't really off the cuff. It's carefully calculated to have an effect. It's what I call thought engineering. I cut down the other guy ... and your mind immediately goes to how much bigger a persona I am. I do it all with surgical skill. Hey, I'm not a novice at this stuff.

WEGO Radio: Is that why you spend so much time insulting and tearing down your opponents?

The Donald: Absolutely ... it's what I do best. That stunt I pulled giving out Lindsay Graham's personal phone number to the media was an instant winner. It gave me lasting credibility as a player in the media. The tweet-o-sphere went crazy over it.

WEGO Radio: Yeah, and why exactly did you do that again?

The Donald: He insulted me. I can't have people insulting me and getting away with it. When I retaliated like that it was my way of saying to the world, "Don't mess with The Donald."

WEGO Radio: So can we expect President Donald Dump to exact revenge against world leaders who might intentionally or unintentionally slight you?

The Donald: Absolutely ... nobody in this world ... and I mean nobody is above the Donald. Anybody who tries to put me down is dead meat. I'm on record now saying that, "Don't mess with The Donald."

WEGO Radio: Don't mess with The Donald? Sounds terrifying. So would you be willing to mobilize America's war machine to get revenge on some world leader who dissed you?

The Donald: We probably wouldn't mobilize the whole war machine ... just enough to make a statement. Or maybe we'd send in a swat team for a surgical strike - taking out the offending party and a few extras for good measure. Just like in the movies.

WEGO Radio: You're beginning to sound like Richard III.

The Donald: Who?

WEGO Radio: He was in that movie - starring Ian McKellen, Annette Bening - he was the King of England, celebrated by Shakespeare for taking out everyone who was a potential threat to his throne.

The Donald: See, that's my point. Shakespeare celebrated him. They're always celebrating the big egos. When I'm President they're are going to be a lot of celebrations ... mostly about me ...

but also some celebrations for our new trade agreements ... our prosperity ... our simpler tax code.

WEGO Radio: Okay since you brought it up ... what about these tax proposals. Seems to me a billionaire like you will pay a lot less in taxes under your plan.

The Donald: Is there something wrong with that?

WEGO Radio: Depends what you consider wrong.

The Donald: Exactly and what poor people consider wrong and what rich people consider wrong are two different things. That's why rich people, like me, are rich.

WEGO Radio: Oh ... I'm beginning to understand what this ego thing is all about ... when your ego gets big enough everything you do and say is right.

The Donald: Now you're learning.

WEGO Radio: But isn't there such a thing as reality? Nobody is always right?

The Donald: You're beginning to understand kid. Being an ego like me is all about creating a reality warp. In any contest it's one ego against another. The ego that's bigger always wins. Because that's what winning is, imposing your will on someone else.

WEGO Radio: That sounds crazy.

The Donald: It is crazy. We live in a crazy world. People don't pay attention to anything long enough to process it. They're too busy flipping between screens and channels. You'll never and I mean never see me start boring people with policy details or proposals. Why?

WEGO Radio: Because you don't have any policy details?

The Donald: I don't have any and I don't need any. All people want to know about me is that I'm amazing ... I'm terrific ... I'm the Donald and I'm doing it my way.

WEGO Radio: But history has not been kind to world leaders who had this "my way or the highway" attitude.

The Donald: Name one instance where history hasn't been kind to that attitude.

WEGO Radio: Let's start with the Vietnam war ... a war that made no sense but took 2 million lives because the smart asses in the state department had huge egos. They thought they were the best and brightest and convinced themselves and everybody else they were right about something that they were wrong about.

The Donald: Exactly ... smart ass Harvard types who didn't know shit because they were in some ivory tower instead of the Trump Tower. I know how to run a campaign and I don't need some sniffle nosed Ivy league, ass kisser to tell me what to say and how to say it.

WEGO Radio: You seem to be getting worked up. It this your ego kicking into gear?

The Donald: My ego is always in gear. I don't need to kick it to start it.

WEGO Radio: Speaking of starting ... what would be your first act as President?

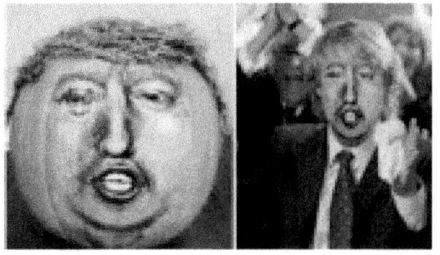

The Donald: Well in terms of redesign, I'd remodel the U. S Capitol building and rename it the National Dumpster. But on a more substantive level, I'd pass an amendment of the U. S. Constitutions to turn America into a corporate enterprise?

WEGO Radio: Why would you do that?

The Donald: You can't get anything done in Congress like it is. They're too many procedural delays ... too many votes. It's totally dysfunctional. With a corporate charter, votes are easy ... each share is one vote ... On every important issue we just poll the shareholders of American Inc, tally up the votes and start getting stuff done ... and make American Great Again.

WEGO Radio: So who would decide who gets shares of America Inc?

The Donald: The market would decide.

WEGO Radio: How?

The Donald: Shares of U. S Inc could be bought by anyone on a public exchange? It would be open to the public - Anyone could buy into the American dream.

WEGO Radio: But only people with money could participate?

The Donald: Yeah ... and ... ?

WEGO Radio: So those with money would rule the world? How is making America a corporate enterprise better than what we have now?

The Donald: Oh we'll still have one man one vote for elections and stuff ... but the people who are elected won't have any power. The power will be with the shareholders of America Inc.

WEGO Radio: Just like it is now – but without the window dressing.

The Donald: Exactly, we will have formalized the arrangement s between wealth and power in society. We'll give it legal status so when Congressmen are bought and sold it will be all right out in the open and entirely legitimate. And by the way, that's why I'm self financing my campaign.

WEGO Radio: Why?

The Donald: So I can make my own decisions, unencumbered by what campaign contributors might otherwise tell me what to do.

WEGO Radio: So there would be no checks and balances in your administration? No one would ever be able to challenge or second guess you as President?

The Donald: That's what being the biggest ego in the world is all about.

WEGO Radio: But what if you're having a bad hair day and start making really bad decisions just because you don't like the way your hair looks?

The Donald: Haven't you been listening? I don't make bad decisions ... all my decisions are right. I'm losing my patience with you. Listen I gotta go.

Why I Support the Donald?

By Lucy Farnhill

Author of "I'm Crazy Over You, Donald"

Each evening at six, when I watch the news and see the Donald there speaking up for America's greatness ... I get the goose bumps. I live vicariously through the Donald's campaign. Honestly my job sucks. I've been doing the same boring thing for 18 years, and the Donald has brought some excitement into my life. I first felt that excitement at the You Can Do It ... motivational seminar when they showed a video of The Donald. He told us  how he had made billions in real estate and Hollywood. I said that's what I want to do in life. But I have bills to pay and I'm not really much to look at ... a tad overweight ... and I'm not sure I would want all that comes with being rich and famous like the Donald ... the parapets, the bodyguards and all that. So I let the Donald do it all for me. I live through him ...

With the Donald at the Hell helm of this ship of state, America will sale through choppy waters to become great again., Simply put Donald Dump has been ordained by fate to save America from itself - from the do nothing Congress - from the criminals who are flooding this country from other shores in Mexico. Yes, the Donald, has his detractors and detractions. Yes there are those who criticize his ideas, tactics, his bankruptcies and his hair. But one thing you cannot belittle - his ego. His ego is beyond criticism and compare. Where else in our society today can you find so much in so little? This book is a testemint to the man behind the ego. He's winner not a whiner. He's a leader not a bleeder. He's our candidate and I support him 110%.

The Ego and the Man

Even his not so subtle critics and others who seem not to hold him in such a high limelight have to admit that Donald Dump's Ego is a thing to behold - in all it's splendor. Okay, maybe Donald Dump' has made a few mistakes in his life. Okay maybe the surgery on his scalp didn't go so good. Okay maybe he's raped a few wives, but now even those wives support his candidacy bolstered by outsized settlement in divorces and other court cases. While we're at it we also want to call out the academic snobs who may think that the type and related fonts we use in this book are big enough for Donald Dumps ego. They say that it's beneath their dignity to read such small type about such a big man. Let's not get snooty.

The real reason we want to go on the record is to put to rest the notion that Donald Dump is a gimmick. Not! We believe that Donald Dump's ego is the real thing and it's just what history ordered. In other words Donald Dump Ego is the real deal? He the authentic second coming of somebody who is truly a person worthy of note and special attention that He has warranted from the mainstream press not withstanding the rot that spews forth from the media pundits? You decide!

Nuff said.

The Donald Dump Enemies List

One of the most amazing things about Donald Trump is how quickly and effectively he disarms his enemies. He's not afraid of picking public fights with media icons, and serious politicians. The whole strategy is strategic. Every time he does it the media eats it up, his supporter go wild and his poll numbers go up. Trump knows that the media feeds on conflict like it's red meat. He's got it out for the lamestream media ... Washington Gridlock ... you name it ... Trump feeds their frustrations with the red meat of insults, taunts, and disparaging remarks. Here's just a partial a list of those who Donald Dump has taken down.

ABCD News - Balanced Reporting By Imbalanced Journalists who worship Mickey Mouse and Donald Duck. They just don't know how smart The Donald is.

Al Bore - Former Veep (Sigh) and President-elect, now a pompous professor type, Hollywood Climate Changing actor, college debating coach, Nobel Peacemaker, (what a joke, and throw in Oboomas award just for laughs); financial advisor with direct ties to Wall Street and their plot to overthrow the government, which they already control and meanwhile is he overweight or what and why doesn't he seek advice from a weight control expert? Al Bore sees Donald Dump as someone who doesn't "Get It" simply because He is adopting a more analytical and scientifically proven approach to the facts about global warming, environmentalism and hunting wolves from helicopters. Mr. Harvard Hot Air Snootiness is tiresome to say the least.

Alan Greenback - Former Chief of Federal Reserve Bored who is still plotting with Wall Street wizards and OBooma boosters to develop a plan to negate the national debt with help from the Congress that so assiduously created the immoral debt in the first place.

Al Friggin - Friggin' liberal comedian, turned U. S. Senator, former white knight of the left and talk show host on "Fair America." He makes jokes about things that are not funny, like Donald Dump's sentence structure and wordage. Okay, Al so you're so smart. How do you pronounce "smartipants?" (like you are!)

Barack Obooma - Needs no introduction as an enemy of all of us. Did you see how he sipped his beer? NoBell NoBama Peace Prize? What? Get a clue Swedes. What's next Superbowl MVP? Ultra liberal intellectual type who gives great speeches, but can he walk the talk when it comes to being a true honest believer in the no nonsense values that Donald Dump represents instead of the inside the beltway type thinking that pervades corporate America and

Wall Street, not to mention how the media distorts The Donald's record and policies. An opportunist!

Barbara Falters - TV Anchorwoman whose penetrating questions can always be counted on to reveal nothing because she won't stoop to interview Donald Dump, because she is afraid that The Donald will show her up with his intelligence, good looks and toughness.

Barbara Boxing - Pugnatious Democrapic Senator from the dissident State of California who champions the fight of the little liberals; leader of the Boxing Rebellion to challenge the electoral college vote tally. MoveOn, Barbara and get with the Paradigm.

Ben Person - Retired neurosurgeon who surged past the Donald in some polls prompting the Donald to go ballistic citing his pathological personality - a condition the Donald says can't be cured.

Billary C. - She thinks she can become the first woman in the White House. She already tried that once but twice got schlonged on the way .... first by her adulterous husband, then by that black dude who smoked cigarettes and gave great speeches, like the Donald does even better. Former First Lady, turned a New York carpetbagger in the U. S. Senate; widely read authoress; then got promoted to secretarial status by Barack Obooma - in a back room deal that nobody has yet investigated, but the Donald will. In her secretarial capacity, she got a frequent flyer package second to none, and power limited only by the U. S. budget deficits and the Chinese negotiators who always take us to the cleaners, and that may be why her pant suits are always rumpled?

Bill Clintstone - Former President of the United States, now a touring author, marriage counselor, world savior, part time librarian and potential First Man in the White House. What?

Bill O'Really - Foxy News Network talking head who flagellates guests on his show with hardball questions and then interrupts so fast that the guest becomes whooped ever before they open their mouth like the time he told Al Friggin to "Shut up. Just shut up" at ABA bookseller event. Friggin didn't and kept wagging his tongue all the way to the U. S. Senate which hey

Minnesota always was a littly wacky with their politicians; remember that wrestler guy and Omidgod what was I talking about ... Oh yes, Bill O'Really ... Oh Really?

The Boston Club - Semi-Respected New England newspaper famed for it's old school connections and strange accents.

Karl Rude – He's the epitome of the Repugnicant establishment. Omniscient White House etiquette expert and political strategist; Once the most powerful and least accountable non-elected official ever in the history of the world, not counting Jesus Christ. More recently has gone off the deep end with his cutting remarks about Donald Dump being a disaster and his non qualifications to be the most powerful person in the world. Like George Bush, who he served as spinmeister for so faithfully long was better qualified than our very own Donald Dump. Yeah, right, Karl!

Colin Powwow – Diplomatic Former Secretary of Stateliness, who presented the Bush Weapons of Mass Distraction (WMD) case to World masterfully– now preparing for a leading role in the upcoming reality TV show, "White House Survivor." He became an official enemy on our list when he opined that Donald Dump was not what we all hope and expect from Presidential hopefuls, by way of qualifications.

Condolessa Nice – Former national security advisor and Secretary of State who tried to bring a feminine perspective to the George B. Wush inner circle. But she is now off into her own world of hobnobbing with old boy networks, which he is now one.

Crookings Institute – Think tank with a penchant for concluding what their funders want to be concluded and doing so with an emphatic flourish. Basically they're all intellectual whores and inside-the-Beltway snobs.

Dan Blather – TV news personality who was moved to tears by the powerful post 9/11 performance of President Geroge B. Wush and moved to jears by his 16 Minutes report on Bush. But what is he now? Certainly not one of us!

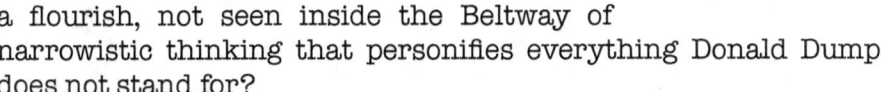

David Brooder – Widely respected, but very dark minded columnist for The Washington Pissed, who is too smart to laugh about what's really happening in the world. If he is so smart why doesn't he understand what really makes a leader like Donald Dump so great and tick like clockwork taking on the media corpse with a flourish, not seen inside the Beltway of narrowistic thinking that personifies everything Donald Dump does not stand for?

Diane Finestew – Let her stew in her own juices of fiscal irresponsibility and prolificacy. If Donald Dump has his way, which He will, California will be expelled from the union of Untied States for bad behavior.

Dick Chicanery – "Smiley" picked himself as part-time Vice President and full-time lobbyist for Hallibirdie Construction Company in Iraq . But this man does not have a fundamentalist Christian bone in his body.

Donald Dumbsfeld – Former Dork of Defense who mastered the art of answering his own questions when asked something else.

But he really was the engineer of the War we didn't want to fight. Donald Dump understands all to well about wars having graduated from NY Military Academy and matriculating in a warlike manner. Which Donald is the real toughie and not a wimp like Dumbsfeld was for always ducking questions tossed like bombs in his face.

Flipper Gore - Former wife of Former Vice President and former star of his own TV sitcom, Flipper. "Really a nice woman, too bad she had to get mixed up with bad company that poor Bore guy.

Foxy News Network - Fair and Balanced news totally .... Yeah ... right ... but unfortunately they don't think Donald Dump has what it takes ... so that is largely without substance, but still the rabid right devours their brand of junkfood journalism as if it were tasty morsels of news McNuggets.

George B. Wush - Some still doubt his sanity. Some day we will all recognize his unique abilities to see the world clearly through his own eyes despite what others might have been seeing differently in the world. It was a testimony to his political vision and courage that he stuck his head out and in.

GEORGE W. BUSH

SEEING THINGS FROM GEORGE'S POINT OF VIEW

George Won't - Establishment conservative syndicated columnist, who just doesn't get the Donald. He has a way of saying what nobody was thinking and doing it in a way that nobody can understand. This is, of course, the mark of a great writer - Not!

Hairy Reid - Democrapic Senate Majority Leader who was always trying to stick it to America. He thinks heath care reform is good for America. Not!

Howard Scream - Democrapic Organizational Man - Famed for his ability to mine Internet for gold and his "Amazing Scream." Heads up the email fundraising program for DNC.

Huck Mukabee - It is difficult to take seriously somebody who has a name so skewered that it is parody ripe, right out of the gate. He purports to be a religiously oriented person, but what exactly is he preaching when it is not in the mainstream of Donaldesque thought? Is he an enemy? Absolutely, because he feels threatened by Donald Dump's fresh breed of change against the older male dominated politics that this country has had enough of, for too long now that a fresh breeze of change has started blowing in the form of Donald Dump.

Jay Limo - Fabulously wealthy, but ultimately misguided and dangerous late night talk show host known for his heavy reliance on laugh tracks, big chins and grins. But he is treading on thin ice when he tries to make fun of Donald Dump with his oh so clever jokes that wouldn't even be funny if he knew what a formidable force Donald Dump is. He singlehandedly brings down late night talk show hosts with his in your face style of response to their not so subtle jokes about his foibles and folksiness.

Jeb P. Wush - Eastern establishment personified - low energy guy. Helped seal President Wush's, - the greatest heist in human history, the Florida Presidential election, and now trying to convince people that the Bush brand will still sell. Nobody's buying it. He deserves to be ignored being the brothers of one of our countries most perplexing Politicians who didn't really help things much as President.

Jerry Foulmouth – Religious Wrong figurehead and poster child for foot-in-mouth disease.

Joe Biddle - Silver tongued and even more silver haired Vice Presidential candidate formerly of U. S. Senate and unpresidential bids for President ....

who was coattailed into the White House on the cape of Barack Obooma's election . But the real questions about Joe Biddle are, "Who does his hair? Why does he still commute by train from Delaware?"

John McPain - Maverick Repugnicant Senator from Arizona who catapulted Saint Sarah into fame with her pick as VEEP candidate. The two developed a lovingly testy relationship that mirrors the love hate relationship of all Repugnicants with Donald Dump and his entourage. Is he the enemy? Well, his legions have done what they can't to try to foil Donald Dump's reputation as a political heavyweight worthy of running the highest office in the land with skill and sagacity.

Jon Stewage – TV Star of The Daily Stew - A delightful concoction of tasty morsels of news McNuggerts that cooks the politicos.

Larry Zing – Cable TV Talk Show host who knows how to hoist himself up by his own suspenders in the Nielsen ratings

Los Angeles Tomes - Respected daily left coast newspaper that somehow manages to survive presenting in-depth news amidst the superficiality of La La Land.

Snit Romney – He remains a formidable enemy of the Donald if for no other reason that a brokered convention might put the Republican nomination in his lap in a political pinch. A promisingly potentialized political opponent with the ageless good looks of a chiseled face upon Mount Rushmore before the fact of chiselment. But do not be deceived by his superficious demeanor. He is lacking-in-depth persona and lives in as many states as he could with many wives who were scuttled about underground to prevent media scrutiny of his fringe Religious so called beliefs and cults.

Molly Ivan – Penetrating Liberal wit and columnist – "Ivan the Terrible" to all conservatives. But she got what she deserved when she died. Death is God's way of telling liberals to shut up!

MoveOn.org - What a name? Why don't they just do what their name says and get the hell out of Dodge. Bunch a wimpy Eastern liberals! Muck um!

Nancy Peloski – Liberal Democrapic House Minority leader seeking to steer the Democrapic ship of state out of the fog towards Obooma's vision of a true socialist state. Talk about enemies... She personifies everything Donald Dump does not stand for.

Newt Gangrene - Aka - Snoot Gingrich: The Professor officially flamed out in Iowa in 2012 ... in the breathtaking span of a few weeks ... true to his words he refused to run a negative campaign and instead just laid the truth on the line by calling Snit Romney a liar on national TV ... truly hates the Snit ... he saw Snit bottoming

out at 25% ... and himself ... well according to the Professor, he's the only electable alternative ... the professor's always right ... right? Former Speaker of the House and architect of the Rapacious Repugnicant "Contract On America" which helped renew Repugnicant faith in their ability to control the masses. He has graduated to green pastures (if you know what I mean) as a DC consultant reaping the rewards of his influence. He is the noted author of books of little note.

Oprah Whimsey - Whimsical daytime talk queen as TV's only extant promoter of the dying art of reading books and living art of dieting. She would be okay except that she's in tight with fellow Chicagoan and the racially tinged occupant of the White House (What does that tell you about so called "American values?") So reluctantly we must put her on our official enemies list even though we like her and she is a woman fighter just like Donald Dump is and aways will be until Donald's campaign carries the day in Washington DC and across the airwaves of America into living rooms.

Pat Bloberson - TV Evangelist and Star of Rapturously Repugnicant Syndicated Show, with a penchant for making outrageous statements. No fan of the Donald and vice versa.

P. Rick Perry: Four years ago he spent $480 per vote in Iowa ... today he's out of money ... out of ideas and out of the race. Now that was a Texas size blunder ... When asked how he saw the race now ... "It's a three horse race ... between Donald Dump, Donald Trump and ... and .... oops ..." One thing's for sure ... the third horse is not him ... he's going back to pasture in Texas. ... but wait ... there's more .... just Tweeted something about South Carolina ... onward and ... and .... and ... and ... oops ..."

Run Paul: The Radical's credentials as a legitimate spoiler severely undermined by his 1% in the polls ... rabid supporters with online fundraising and Facebook presence second only to the Snit .... the plot sickens.

The New York Tombs – New York rag respected for its obits both of the living and the dead; their motto, "All the news that will fit in print."

The Washington Pissed - DC newspaper famed for its determined digging into matters that are guaranteed to arouse acrimony on both sides of the aisle.

50 Amazing Things That
The Donald Really Did Say

1. "Why aren't we smart? We used to be brilliant.

2. Part of the beauty of me is that I am very rich.

3. When was the last time you saw a Chevrolet in Tokyo?

4. I'm not a schmuck.

5. I do not wear a rug. My hair is one hundred percent mine.

6. Let me tell you, I'm a really smart guy.

7. Sometimes your best investments are the ones you don't make.

8. A certificate of live birth is not the same thing by any stretch of the imagination as a birth certificate.

9. My fingers are long and beautiful, as, it has been well been documented, are various other parts of my body.

10. Some people call me lucky, but I know better.

11. I love beautiful women, and beautiful women love me. It has to be both ways.

12. They're sending people who have lots of problems. They bring in drugs, they bring in crime, they're rapists. I assume some are good people. It's got to stop, and it's got to stop fast.

13. I have a great relationship with the blacks. I've always had a great relationship with the blacks.

14. Laziness is a trait in blacks.

15. A well-educated black has a tremendous advantage over a well-educated white in terms of the job market. I think sometimes a black may think they don't have an advantage or this and that... I've said on one occasion, even about myself, if I were starting off today, I would love to be a well-educated black, because I believe they do have an actual advantage.

16. I am the least racist person there is. And I think most people that know me would tell you that. I am the least racist.

17. The concept of global warming was created by and for the Chinese in order to make U.S. manufacturing non-competitive.

18. It's like taking the New England Patriots and Tom Brady and have them play your high school football team. That's the difference between our leaders and China's leaders.

19. My twitter has become so powerful that I can actually make my enemies tell the truth.

20. It's freezing and snowing in New York—we need global warming!

21. People are tired of these nice people.

22. This very expensive GLOBAL WARMING bullshit has got to stop. Our planet is freezing, record low temps, and our GW scientists are stuck in ice.

23. .@ariannahuff is unattractive both inside and out. I fully understand why her former husband left her for a man—he made a good decision.

24. By the way, I have great respect for China. I have many Chinese friends. They live in my buildings all over the place.

25. I will build a great wall — and nobody builds walls better than me, believe me —and I'll build them very inexpensively. I will build a great, great wall on our southern border, and I will make Mexico pay for that wall. Mark my words.

26. Free trade is terrible. Free trade can be wonderful if you have smart people. But we have stupid people.

27. Why is Obama playing basketball today? That is why our country is in trouble!

28. How come every time I show anger, disgust or impatience, enemies say I had a tantrum or meltdown—stupid or dishonest people?

29. Black guys counting my money! I hate it. The only kind of people I want counting my money are little short guys that wear yarmulkes every day.

30. In order to get elected, @BarackObama will start a war with Iran.

31. Sadly, because president Obama has done such a poor job as president, you won't see another black president for generations!

32. I've always been a fan of Steve Jobs, especially after watching Apple stock collapse w/out him—but the yacht he built is truly ugly.

33. An 'extremely credible source' has called my office and told me that @BarackObama's birth certificate is a fraud.

34. I'll tell you, it's Big Business. If there is one word to describe Atlantic City, it's Big Business. Or two words—Big Business.

35. We have nobody in Washington that sits back and said, you're not going to raise that fucking price.

36. Rosie O'Donnell's disgusting both inside and out. You take a look at her, she's a slob. She talks like a truck driver, she doesn't have her facts, she'll say anything that comes to her mind....I mean she's basically a disaster.

37. Our great African American President hasn't exactly had a positive impact on the thugs who are so happily and openly destroying Baltimore!

38. More votes equals a loss...revolution!

39. You know, it really doesn't matter what [the media] write as long as you've got a young and beautiful piece of ass.

40. Well, somebody's doing the raping, Don! I mean somebody's doing it! Who's doing the raping? Who's doing the raping?

41. The more you know, the more you realize how much you don't know.

42. The second-greatest day of a man's life is the day he buys a yacht, but the greatest day of a man's life is the day he sells it.

43. Buy companies only when you understand what they do.

44. All of the women on 'The Apprentice' flirted with me—consciously or unconsciously. That's to be expected.

45. I get up, take a shower and wash my hair. Then I read the newspapers and watch the news on television, and slowly the hair dries. It takes about an hour. I don't use the blow dryer. Once it's dry I comb it. Once I have it the way I like it—even though nobody else likes it—I spray it and it's good for the day.

46. Sorry losers and haters, but my IQ is one of the highest—and you all know it! Please don't feel so stupid or insecure, it's not your fault.

47. And did you notice that baby was crying through half of the speech and I didn't get angry? Not once. Did you notice that? That baby was driving me crazy. I didn't get angry once because I didn't want to insult the parents for not taking the kid out of the room!

48. I think the only difference between me and the other candidates is that I'm more honest and my women are more beautiful.

49. It's amazing how people can talk about me but I'm not allowed to talk about them.

50. In life you have to rely on the past, and that's called history.

Can the Donald Make America Great Again?

By Buzzy Beal

Founder and CEO
Real Estate Typhoons for the Donald

To sum it up in just one word, "You bet he can." The Donald will rise America up by it's bootstraps once again. He's not one for modesty and his vision is anything but a modest goal. There are seven reasons why I'm absolutely certain Donald Dump is ordained by fate to be the one to make America great again.

1. He's smart! You know this because he's a billionaire.

2. He has what it takes. Plus he knows how to negotiate a deal.

3. He tells it like it is and he gets things done.

4. He knows business and he understands the value of a brand.

5. He knows the right people to get things done.

6. He knows how the media works, and it's not a pretty picture.

7. He'll send all those criminals from Mexico back home.

Part III

Actual
Reality

Dealing With Donald Trump Reality Warp

We are rapidly approaching "reckoning of sorts." Perhaps we have already reached it. The data is unclear. A "reckoning" is the moment at which society, as a whole, starts to totally freak out and common sense soon becomes an anachronism. Then we all descend into a dark space - new kind of reality warp. Donald Trump's campaign and all its accompanying mania provides us with a frightening glimpse of what might lie at the bottom of this descent – if we do nothing about it.

What Donald Trump has done to politics is not good, but we've got to see it for what it is. That is … we need to deal with this reality warp. Now even key players in the Republican party power structure are considering an unthinkable reality … what happens to the party and the country if he wins?

Yes, we need to confront a harsh reality here. Yes, Donald Trump is a ego inflated buffoon. He's an entertainer. He has no serious solutions to the myriad problems that our society faces. He's in this thing for himself. He's not a good person. The only reason he's still in business is because his bankers realized that the Donald was worth more to them whole, than if he's in bankruptcy.

If Donald Trump were applying for almost any other job in the world he wouldn't get it. Why don't we as a country get it? Why do we give him credence for the most important job in the world? He's not even remotely qualified to be President. …. and yes Jeb Bush is right – *Donald Trump is a jerk.* But he's a jerk that people keep talking about. This is what he wants. So what are we going to do about this? What's the answer to the Donald Trump conundrum? Simple ...

Donald Dump is the answer to Donald Trump!

What Are We Going To Do About this Clown?

The rise of the *Donald Trump Phenomenon* begs the obvious question that sooner or later we're going to have to face up to:

What now?

This isn't our first encounter with this kind of challenge. When John McCain picked Sarah Palin as his running mate we all were confronted with the possibility that Saint Sarah might actually be one heartbeat away from the Presidency. In comparison to what we have now, that was fun and games. If the Donald wins, he'll actually be in the oval office, sitting there cluelessly with his finger on the button. This is serious business - no more fun and games.

We absolutely must do everything we can to insure that Donald Trump's brand of *Making America Great Stupid Again* never comes to pass. It would be a complete, total and unmitigated disaster. He has absolutely no experience in office - any political office. He's not even remotely qualified to be the most powerful person on the planet. He's bankrupted four companies. But, so far he's proved to be impervious to all attacks. We need a plan to puncture the Donald's balloon. I implore you - stand up for America - do what you can – anything - to de-activate Donald Trump [22] … talk to your friends … and of course, buy the book and wear the t-shirt. Buy hundreds and pass them out to strangers on the street. Share it all with friends on Facebook and Twitter. This is your opportunity to shine. You too can become part of an historic movement. Our sole mission is to puncture the Donald's balloon by marketing the anti-Trump brand - the *Donald Dump* brand. To get a handle on what's it this is about read on. This is serious business. The fate of the free world depends on it.

Anybody But The Donald

From a far out political galaxy called reality, the entire Donald Trump phenomenon can be viewed as a titanic struggle between two opposing factions – them and us. We're the force. They're the farce. They're the members of Donald Trump's Reality Warp and we're exposing them as imposters.

We're the heroic members of the Donald Trump De-activation Society [23] out to right the wrong. We're the aghast onlookers. We sit up in the galactic stands looking down at the Donald Trump Reality Warp shaking our heads in disbelief. *How can this be happening?* … we ask. Then flip the channel … surf to another Website or check our cellphone for ball scores or texts.

And that's the nub of the problem. Too few members of the Donald Trump De-activation Society are really tuned in. We're actively inactive members. Whereas, the crazies on the the other side, are maniacal in their support of the Donald. To them, the Donald fills in the empty spaces of their lives. And … we just hope that Donald Trump will eventually go away - ***but he's not going away.***

At the Donald Trump De-Activation Society, we recognize this conundrum. We're on a mission – to activate the inactive members of the Donald Trump De-Activation Society. Yes, it's a paradox. It's a befuddlement - but deeper truths of our existence seldom proceeds in a straight line of linear logic. We're not pushing any other candidate. Our ideal candidate is ABTD - *Anybody But The Donald.*

---

[23] facebook.com/DonaldTrumpDeactivationSociety

The Goal of the Donald Trump De-Activation Society

So - to sum up – the goal of the Donald Trump De-Activation Society is simple - to get Donald Trump to go away - to de-activate himself. That's our entire raison d'être. It's our reason for being - our reason for living and once achieved it will be our reason for dying.

The strategy of the Donald Trump Activation Society [24] is to inflate Donald Trump's ego so big that it eventually pops - or poops. That's our dream - to see that bubble that defines the reality warp that of Donald Trump's supporters go pop in the night like a bottle of Champagne. Our goal is to get Donald Trump to go away - to self destruct - to never be seen or heard from again - not on Twitter - not on Fox … not on CNBC … or any network any cable channel, any blog, any conversation anyplace - just go away Donald. We've had enough of your traveling show. We've seen your circus tricks and clown act enough. And most assuredly we don't want to see you sitting in the Oval Office.

Our goal isn't ignominy. We just want The Donald to go away. If he can find any dignity to take with him, that's fine - just go away. Donald, take all the spare dignity and self respect you can find in your bulging pockets or under the seat of your private plane … just go away any way you can … evaporate … vanish … disappear ... be gone with yourself … JUST GO AWAY! Donald ...

24 facebook.com/DonaldTrumpDeactivationSociety

Categories of Membership in DTDS

The Donald Trump De-Activation Society has three classes of members - depending on how they view Donald Trump Reality Warp.

Active Members: They're the actual supporters of Donald Trump. They've catalyzed this entire Donald Dump phenomenon. Without them Donald Trump would be a blowhard in the wind. They're the visible ones at rallies with signs and bullhorns. These stalwart members have actually given Donald Trump some semblance of credibility - at least as measured by that modern day anointment ointment - the polls.

Charter Members: Not all *DTRW Members* confine their activities to the circus. Some pose as real people and have real jobs. Many *Charter Members of DTRW* actually have paying jobs in the media and feel they owe a debt of gratitude to *The Donald* for giving them something fresh to write about. The Donald has been a boon to industry in that way. In a business where success is defined by ratings, Donald Trump is a roaring success.

Ex-officio Members: *Ex-officio Members* are not as active, but they enjoy watching this circus. They only see Donald Trump through reality warp. Some entered this reality warp between bites of popcorn and gulps of beer while watching *The Apprentice* for the Nth time. Some entered *DT Reality Warp* while attending a DT branded motivational seminar. Some came through the emptiness of their own lives … using the Donald as a surrogate for the success and excitement their lives lack. Some entered through media overload. One day they just gave up and said, *Okay Donald, you're real - now what?* Some entered nodding off while watching the evening news groggily mumbling, *I like what this guy says.* without paying attention to any of the words he was actually using to cast his spell…. now on with the show.

Solving the Mystery of Our Age

A mystery that's been perplexing me for some time now - ever since Donald Trump declared for President and shot up to the top of the polls. I can understand why the Donald is running - that's easy - to increase the value of the Donald Trump brand and to massage his own ego. But what I don't understand is the mentality of the people who are supporting him.

The whole thing blows my mind. Trump is a guy who owns real estate and charges people rents that are high enough to make him wads of money. Don't people realize that Trump is one of the class of rich bastards who are ripping them off?

Trump plasters his name and ego on everything he can and then charges people to put his name on what they're selling. Macy's actually pays Trump to put the Trump name on ties imported from Mexico, who he says are sending us their criminals.

How do we as a society counter this kind of crazed behavior? Wait, I've got an idea. Let's plant weeds in the Trump garden? What if we start inserting the name Donald Dump every place that the Donald is planting his own name. Will it start registering with people? *Will they realize that something is amiss in the world of politics if every time the hear the name Donald Trump their thoughts automatically revert to the image of Donald Dump instead?*

We don't know, but it's worth a try. Nothing else seems to be working to tame the ego of this bombastic boor.

Donald Dump
Strategic Plan

"Own a Piece of the Donald"

www.DonaldDump.top

A Sensible Alternative to Throwing Your
Money Away at Other Politicians

The Farcical Force Be With Us

To deal with a surreal character like Donald Trump we need a surreal plan - carefully crafted to get us out of the surreal mess Donald Trump has got us in. Our plan starts with the farcical force. It's an amorphous and pervasive force that emanates from an intergalactic source known as *The Donald Trump De-Activation Society*. The force has but one objective – to puncture *The Donald's* balloon sized ego. To accomplish this noble mission .... **The farcical force will** focus it's energy on a very big target - an irresistible target - the Donald Trump brand - and create an equal and opposite force in the form of *The Anti-Trump Brand.*

The Anti-Trump force will consolidate opposing forces some of whom are very strange bedfellows - Republicans scared the Donald might get the nomination - Latinos, Muslims, and those offended by his gutter style of politics - anyone with a lick of sense - anyone who sees the Donald as demagogue who manipulates the media by stoking fears and appealing to base human instincts.

The Value of the Anti-Trump Brand

The Donald Trump Brand is arguably the most powerful personal brand in the universe today. Before the Donald announced his candidacy he valued his personal brand at over $3 billion. With nearly 24/7 Trump news coverage for months now, the value of Trump brand may have actually appreciated during this campaign season. If the Trump brand is now worth well over $3 billion, imagine how valuable the anti-Trump brand might be. Remember, a lot more people don't like him than do?

Our mission is part business venture, part political crusade and part therapy. We view an investment of our time or money in the *Donald Dump Phenomenon* to be a more efficacious use of capital than political contributions. We believe that using modern tools of technology and guerrilla marketing tactics we can create

DONALD TRUMPET

an anti-Trump brand of significant value in a very short period of time while helping people to feel better about themselves by puncturing the Donald's oversized ego.

Beyond the considerable revenue potential from sale of anti-Trump branded content and merchandise, let's consider the value of political influence. Whatever influence Donald Trump loses through the public puncturing of the Donald Trump balloon, is someone's else's gain. What might other candidates and their donors might be willing to invest in an orchestrated takedown of the Donald? In the last Presidential election both Obama and Mitt Romney raised close to a billion dollars to finance their campaigns. This came from people who aren't in the habit of investing their money without expecting something return. They know that *Democracy is not a spectator sport.*

Something Must Be Done

There is now serious talk in Republican circles about what to do in the event that the Donald wins the nomination. *The Wall Street Journal* recently reported, *Some of the highest-ranking Republicans in Congress and some of the party's wealthiest and most generous donors have balked at trying to take down Mr. Trump ... Almost everyone in the party's upper echelons agrees **something must be done**, and almost no one is willing to do it.* [25]

If they won't do it - than aided by the force, we will. We will puncture the Donald's balloon both literally and figuratively by creating creating a lean, mean guerrilla marketing and merchandising operation, with a dab of advertising, a pinch of promotion and a social media presence worthy of a movie release. Our goal of puncturing Donald Trump's balloon is more than metaphor. Our marketing strategy builds upon the most sophisticated techniques of media persuasion by using repetition through celebrity based visuals leaving - an indelible image in people's minds. Puncturing The Donald's balloon size ego is both a mental and visual image. Here's how this powerful visual will be implanted in citizen's and voter's minds everywhere:
• Ads for Donald Dump balloons flood the Web - are sold everywhere.
• Celebrities take selfies of themselves puncturing the balloon.
• Videos link to the Donald Dump merch on the DD Facebook page.
• Videos of people puncturing DD balloons go viral.
• Citizens, young and old feel engaged -
• They feel the force with them as they puncture the Donald's ego.
• "Puncture Parties" become the ice bucket challenge for politics.
• It taps into a "Burning Man" type hunger to tap creative urges.
• It all culminates with the National Donald Dump Puncture Party with image of the Donald's balloon popping is implanted in minds everywhere on the weekend before the Republican Convention.

---

[25] http://www.nytimes.com/2015/12/02/us/politics/wary-of-donald-trump-gop-leaders-are-caught-in-a-standoff.html?_r=0

The Caricature and the Slogan

Donald Dump... Making America ~~Great~~ Stupid Again

With this slightly bastardized name change and the trailing tag line, we're essentially dumbing down the Donald's message even more than the Donald does. What could be simpler than encapsulating everything we don't like about Donald Trump into two words - **Donald Dump?** [26] These two magical words - Donald Dump - can easily be confused, mingled, substituted or otherwise implanted in people's minds - as code for the takedown of the real Donald Trump brand. That's the goal - to create a reflex response in people's minds. Whenever they hear the name Donald Trump they'll  automatically make the mental switch to the image that Donald Dump conjures up. Even if we fail, we win. If the Donald somehow manages to win the nomination or even the Presidency, we've got that much more time to take potshots an embellish the parody. The Donald Dump brand is an intelligent brand precisely because it basically reduces the attack on the Donald to essence. All marketers know this simple fact - the simpler the message the larger the potential audience.

---

[26] Splinter groups who might prefer names like Donald Chump, or Donald Skunk are of course welcome in the anti-Trump coalition.

Target Markets

Too numerous to mention here. Everywhere you look - another group has been offended byTrump and a coalition is taking shape.   For starters, here are just a few:

• Opposing Republican Candidates who have been insulted and belittled by Donald Trump - Jeb Bush, Ben Carson, Marco Rubio, Rand Paul, Carly Fiorina … did I leave anyone out?

• Women who are offended by his sexist attitude and demeaning remarks towards other women.

• Latinos - Mexicans - Muslims - Asians - Blacks … essentially anyone who isn't white male and either rich or wanting to be rich.

• Anybody else who opposes the rise of xenophobia in America.

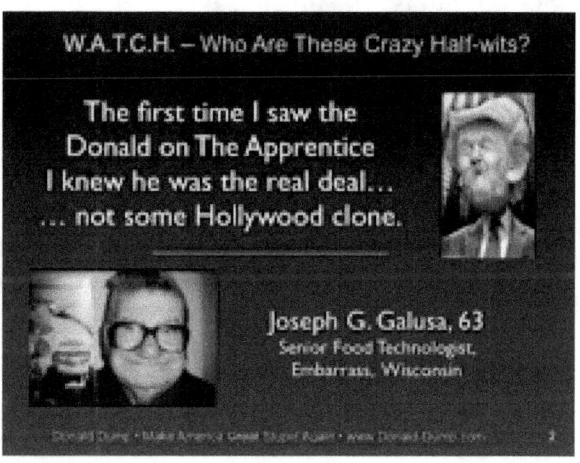

• Reporters, bloggers, pundits and other media types hungry for a new way to present Donald Trump in a new light.

• Young people - especially college students who can bring their own creative talents, tech savvy and abundant energy to this noble venture.

Put it all together and you've got perhaps the greatest market opportunity in America today. It's the golden opportunity to denigrate, mock, be-little, and otherwise capitalize on the essential stupidity of the Donald Trump phenomenon.   That's the challenge and the opportunity - to put together of coalition of anti-Trump forces - which likely will consist of some very strange bedfellows.

Market Size

It's difficult to imagine a larger market and more receptive audience for what we have to sell - the anti-Trump brand. It's so large that in Trump-Type terminology it's *Yuuuuuge*. It's enormous, … it's immense ... large ... big, big, big … great ... massive ... colossal ... prodigious ... gigantic … gargantuan ... mammoth ... and monumental.

Now, let's take a look at the numbers. There are almost 320 million Americans, but only sixty percent or just about 200 million vote in Presidential elections. This 200 million is roughly equally divided between Republicans and Democrats. Of the 100 million Republicans, approximately 1 in 4 says they currently favor the Donald. Extrapolating from current polls, and being very generous, at most 50 million Americans are in his camp - the likely number is is much lower since voter preferences are highly fluid.

That leaves well over 270 million Americans who are potential consumers for the Donald Dump branded content and products. If just one in three citizens in our potential market pays attention to our content the potential advertising revenues are enormous. If one in a hundred donates or spends just an average of $10 on Donald Dump branded merchandise and material, our revenues from merchandise will exceed $300 million. Even if we fall short of our targets, a few hundred million ain't bad for something that will be so much fun to watch.

The DD Guerrilla Marketing Campaign

1. Ubiquity - Everywhere there's a camera following the Donald on the campaign trail, somewhere in the background or the crowd you will find Donald Dump's emissaries engaged in guerrilla marketing:
• donning the signature Red - Donald Dump cap,
• wearing the red, white and blue Donald Dump t-shirt and
• waving the Donald Dump signs and placards.

2. Donald Trump De-Activation Society - It's the official "organization" behind this effort, with regular meetups and online collaboration and chapters on college campuses, and in communities all across America. Imagine:
• strategy sessions in pubs with creative ideas flowing with each gulp of beer,
• online networks to accelerate viral sharing of photos and videos,
• a petition drive to assemble a massive email list of Trump detractors.
• whatever else that strikes the bell with our base.

3. Viral Online Sharing - A steady stream of short, shareable and pithy Tweets, Facebook posts banners specifically designed for viral distribution will emanate from DTAS central and be disseminated through Donald Dump affiliates online Soon existing anti-Trump networks start collaborating and embellishing the themes that underpin the Donald Dump De-Activation Society.

4. W.A.T.C.H. - (Who Are These Crazy Half-wits) – The Donald Dump YouTube channel and video producer - featuring mock interviews with The Donald as well as *the crazies* who have bought into the Donald Trump Brand.

5. A.D.D.A. – (Ask Donald Dump Anything) - The Donald holds forth on everything on Quora, Reddit and other forums. Spurring mainstream media articles blog, posts from political bloggers and virulent attacks from conservative commentators and right wing political hacks. Some produced in written form, other as podcasts on Donald Dump radio and some scripted in videos.

6. TV Attack Ads - The ad buys will be strategic and surgically placed - broadcast less for their direct audience reach and more for indirect sharing on the Web as videos and that provide fodder for the media pundits. The ads return much more than their cost in Web media exposure because they're so good and so different. Example - *Send in the Clown* - a two minute musical parody of Judy Collins *Send in the Clowns* - as background track to visuals of the Donald's greatest moods and mimes. (See appendix)

7. Selling Donald Dump - The Book - 178 pages of sheer delight. It provides the base material and talking points to all operatives working through all the local *Donald Trump De-Activation Society* chapters.

8. Aggressive Publicity Outreach and Outrage - Aggressive contact with key political editors and writers cultivating relationships that provide unique scoops. It's difficult to imagine a more receptive media environment for a venture. Most startups struggle to get any reporter to pay attention to or understand what they're trying to sell. No such problem here. Everybody knows of the Donald and most reporters are stymied by the Donald's staying power. Most are concerned about the Donald and what he represents in politics. They're receptive to pitches that give them a fresh approach and to give expression to their fears about the Donald's candidacy. News coverage of the *Donald Dump Phenomenon* also provides reporters with a way to break out of their straight-jacket of reporting convention.

9. D.D.T. – (Donald Dump Translates) – This is but one of our original Donald Dump memes - content designed for share-ability The Donald's enormous ego shines forth as he interprets the words of the world's great philosophers. Produces as mounted images or caricature based videos.

10. Donald Dump Video - Shorts featuring interviews with the crazies, and much more than we can even imagine now. We give video producers a platform and let them run with the caricature, the slogan and the themes.

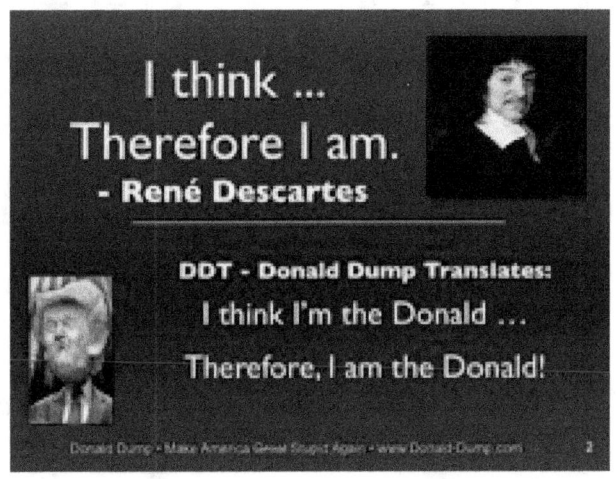

11. Donald Dump Radio - Political chatter, sketches, parodies, interviews - The Daily Show in audio form.

12. Donald Dump Podcast - A weekly roundup of the latest and greatest Donald Dump news and opinion in audio form downloaded right into you car stereo system, computer or cellphone.

13. Donald Dump Mercantile: You name it - we'll find a way to put Donald Dump's name on it and sell it. Imagine, Donald Dump hats, bumperstickers, yard signs, ties, ice cream, underwear, popcorn and much more - all providing that all important brand impressions – a veritable feast of free media exposure. Wherever a crowd or a camera goes with the Donald - Donald Dump operatives will be highly visible.

The National Donald Dump De-Activation and Puncture Party

Mark Your Calendar for July 15 - July 17, 2016

The weekend between the Republican and Democratic Conventions, July 22-24, 2016, an amazing spectacle called The National Donald Dump De-Activation and Puncture Party, will take place virtually and in select locations around the U.S.A. It's an opportunity for clear minded people like us to let loose about Donald Trump. It's our chance to puncture Donald Trumps ego sized balloon in advance of the national Republican and Democratic Conventions. This epochal event will serve as a truly ~~historical~~ hysterical organizing vehicle for something so grand … that … well … even we can't imagine what it might become.

Yes, it's a crazy idea … crazy good. Sometimes crazy is the only appropriate response to a system that has gone crazy on us … as Donald Trump's America has done. *The National Donald Dump Puncture Party* will be a Donald Trump themed parody culminating in a theatre of the absurd. Students and other slightly touched participants, will play the caricatures of Trump supporters and of course The Donald himself. These caricatures will all inflate the Donald's ego sized balloon until it can hold no more hot and and explodes before a national audience. It will be Burning Man, the Ice Bucket Challenge and Saturday Night live all rolled into one.

There will be music, skewered speeches, bastardized media interviews in one huge and over-the-top parody of Donald Trump. It's political theatre for the Internet age. There will be live Webcasts of campus events, local Donald Dump Puncture Parties, all around the country. Facebook groups, Twitter news feeds and YouTube postings and major media outreach. Anyone with a wit and a way can participate. Get creative. Use your wits to register your opposition to politics as usual. Our target? Of course - The Donald.

The buildup to the DDPP will continue through the Spring and Summer of 2016 using social networks and YouTube videos, photoshopped images, T-shirts, bumperstickers - all the standard and non standard paraphernalia of political campaigning.

On this localized, national stage, the DDPP will be programmed for viral growth. The disenchanted and disenfranchised can voice their frustrations in a wry way that detracts major media attention. Our goal is to engage those, who are currently feel disenfranchised by the prevailing political equation.

Just like Donald Trump's real rallies, the National Donald Dump Puncture Party will be strong on bombast and political vacuousness. Speakers will mouth political platitudes like they're Trump-isms. Watch crowds will go berserk over the stupidity of self-serving political ~~prophets~~ profits and media pundits. Sop up the showmanship as if it were real political spectacle. Delegates will cast their votes for the most vapid candidate and we will have accomplished everything that was accomplished in Donald Trump's real campaign … nothing at all.

Asking the Hard Questions of Donald Dump

The following interview intended to disinfect the toxic spray of words that Donald Trump has been releasing through the airwaves and social media. This is critical. Donald Trumps brand of puffed up chicanery is deadly. It kills intelligent discussion … and worse of all it's gets into everything - so that soon all the media pundits become mesmerized not by the Donald but by how their own numbers soar when they cover the Donald … the clicks and audience members and the hits keep on coming. Why? Because they're getting by the other media lemmings who are covering what the Donald says and does. So what the Donald thinks becomes barometer against which everything else in the campaign is measured. Political pundits pass judgement on the other candidates on the basis of how what they said played in the polls and ratings against what the Donald said.

It's a sad situation and dangerous state of affairs in both politics and the media. Donald Trump understands the incestuous relationship between the two - perhaps better than any other candidate in recent times. That's no accident. Donald Trump is a creature of the media - a like huge insect now clawing his way – outrageous statement by outrageous statement – into the upper stratosphere of politics. This insect needs to be stopped and this new strain of DDT (See Appendix) is specially prepared in the test tubes of my mind to counteract what the Real Donald Thinks.

Donald Trump understands that the media above all else is a business that lives and dies by the numbers. He knows that the first thing each celebrity anchor checks after the broadcast is the number of listeners or viewers. Donald Trump understands that his provocations will help the anchors, the bloggers, the talking heads and the jaded pundits get an audience so he's always on their radar and always on their want list. Donald Trump is a wanted man and that's just the way he wants it. But pundits don't ask the hard questions - so the Rogue Writer will.

Donald Dump Exclusive!

The Rogue Writer Interviews The Rogue Candidate

Rogue Writer: Let's start with a very simple question: what do you really stand for?

Donald Dump: Haven't we been over this before? I stand for the Donald Dump brand. And the Donald Dump brand is what stands for me. Which by the way is appreciating in value at amazing rates.

Rogue Writer: How strong is your word?

Donald Dump: As strong as it needs to be in a particular situation. Let's be honest - everybody breaks their word in business and politics. If you're not good at breaking your word you shouldn't be in the game.

Rogue Writer: So are honest people operating at a competitive disadvantage in the world today?

Donald Dump: If they don't know how the game is played they are. If they don't know how business works yes they are. If they don't know the rules of the game they shouldn't be playing.

Rogue Writer: Aren't most of the laws in this country supposed to protect people from this kind of thing?

Donald Dump: You're naivety is charming. You open any book at regs that govern Wall Street. In the small print you'll will find the greatest compendium of obfuscation the world has ever known.

Rogue Writer: So what are the laws in this country for?

Donald Dump: We have laws to make it appear that the game is fair. There's a reason lawyer and regulators write such complex stuff. They do it so nobody can understand what they're saying. And in the unlikely chance that some regulator does understand it, there's enough wiggle room to come out smelling like a rose. That's what business is about today. I understand this better than anyone else and that's why running for President.

Rogue Writer: If others candidates for President actually told the truth would they be at a competitive disadvantage to you?

Donald Dump: None of them are that dumb. Some of them are pretty stupid … especially that guy from Texas .. Wazhisname - P. Rick Perry. He can't even remember his own name. You'll never see me like that … Oops … he says … What a bozo?

Rogue Writer: Speaking of Bozos, did you read that in San Francisco they're selling Bozo like Pinatas that look like you.

Donald Dump: Sound like enterprising young men. If you see them tell them to get in touch with the Donald. I might hire them and send them a check that gives them a real job.

Rogue Writer: I'm sure they'll love working for the man.

Donald Dump: Everybody who works for me loves me, because I send them their paycheck.

Rogue Writer: So is writing the paycheck the ultimate power in our world today?

Donald Dump: You bet it is. That and your power to borrow. The United States is the most powerful nation in the world today because of our creditworthiness. Smart businessmen all over the world invest in America because they know their money is safe with us. They know we're good for out debts - just like the Donald is.

Rogue Writer: Before you'll stiff them in bankruptcy court?

Donald Dump: Let's get off this bankruptcy trip. But I'll tell you this. I've looked at the numbers for the U. S government - and they're not pretty. Our national debt has doubled every 10 years for the last five decades. Technically we're in bankruptcy. But I don't make a big point of talking about that because whatever the Donald says carries such force in financial circles that it could shake up the markets. And I don't want that because I'm heavily invested - in the markets as well as golf courses, hotels, office towers. All that would be affected if I talked to much about the reality of this country's financial crisis.

Rogue Writer: I get it ... so we need the Donald to steer us through the rough financial waters that are ahead. What's the secret to coming out like a rose in bankruptcy like you did?

Donald Dump: No question about it - good lawyers - and I've got the best. Really good lawyers shine in bankruptcy. It's that simple. But can we get over this bankruptcy thing? You seem fixated on it. Get over it. It's done.

Rogue Writer: I'm just trying to understand how you think - to get inside your head ...

Donald Dump: Stop … don't even think about getting inside my head. Nobody gets inside my head except the Donald.

Rogue Writer: Okay, let's take a different approach. What are some of your ideas for the Presidency?

Donald Dump: I like the idea of remodeling the Capitol Building .. making it taller so it better utilizes the vertical space… letting more light in the building and then renaming it - something like *The National Dumpster* - so it better describes what those losers do all day.

Rogue Writer: So now you're going after Congress?

Donald Dump: Listen, everybody knows about the gridlock. Am I telling you something new? Those guys talk out of both sides of their mouth - then cut a deal that rewards their campaign donors. They dignify it all by calling it "compromise." What they're really doing is selling themselves to the highest bidder.

Rogue Writer: What do you think about Citizen's United?

Donald Dump: It opened up the floodgates. Personally I don't care about Citizen United because I've got plenty of money to self-finance. But players like the Koch brothers are having a lot of fun with Citizen United.

Rogue Writer: So this that what Democracy is all about, these days. - courting the players and trying to get them to part with some of their money?

Donald Dump: Where've you been? Of course it is. Am I telling you something you don't already know? I'm not a compromiser and I get a lot done. I just apply my leverage.

Rogue Writer: But business is fundamentally different from government. In business you have ownership structure to define how decisions are made. Government is all about the interplay of ideology and constituencies translating to votes?

Donald Dump: Listen, I've got the biggest constituency out there - everybody who watched and loved "The Apprentice" - all the people who bow at the alter of the Donald Dump brand. They love me because I know how to do the dance better than any of the others - I've changed the whole choreography of campaigning.

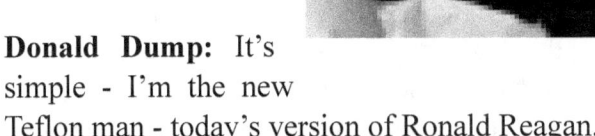

Rogue Writer: Yeah and everybody is mystified but how you do it.

Donald Dump: It's simple - I'm the new Teflon man - today's version of Ronald Reagan.

Rogue Writer: I know it … everybody knows it … but nobody tries to do anything about it … except maybe Bernie Sanders?

Donald Dump: Is that Colonel Sanders a hoot? I love it when he pounds the podium and starts going berserk. He's drawing almost as many people to his events as I draw.

Rogue Writer: So should other candidates concerned because Bernie Sanders is rousing up the passions of people who feel the country has been taken over by the rich? Are you one of those rich people?

Donald Dump: We're not taking over the country - we already took it over. That's why I'm running for President - to consolidate our gains. Remember, I've made a lot of people rich.

Rogue Writer: But why should the people who are being exploited vote for the one of the one's who's exploiting them?

Donald Dump: Your naivety kills me. Poor people don't know they're getting exploited by rich people.

Rogue Writer: Why is that?

Donald Dump: Because rich people own all the television stations, the newspapers, the radio stations the Internet Websites that control their minds. We own the beauty pageants, all the screens and the voice that so many people are addicted to watching. We even own the book publishers. And publishers decide who is smart and who is stupid, but whose books they publish and promote. So rich people bombard poor people crafty advertisements, sports scores and statistics out the kazoo – we push celebrity gossip and all the other forms of junk food journalism that distract poor people from the essential reality that they've getting screwed by the system.

Rogue Writer: You sound like Bernie Sanders now.

Donald Dump: I like the Colonel. He's created a great brand for himself selling chicken and tacos. Bernie Sanders is right about most of his *Cluck Cluck* stuff. The only differences between him and me are 1) that I'm richer than him - way richer 2) I don't do knee jerk responses to hot button liberal issues and 3) I'm better looking than he is - which, by the way, is the way most people decide who to vote for.

Rogue Writer: So policies and political philosophy have nothing to do with it. By the way, what is your political philosophy?

Donald Dump: I don't have a political philosophy. Philosophy is for people who have too much time on their hands. I'm too busy making a success of myself to think about why I'm doing it.

Rogue Writer: Why are the cards all stacked against the little guy in our society?

Donald Dump: Listen, I've got a campaign to run. I don't have time for that left wing wacko stuff. I'm too busy building the Donald Dump brand into the juggernaut that it is - so nobody will ever mistake me for a little guy.?

Rogue Writer: But isn't it the role of government to represent all the people - not just the rich.

Donald Dump: Where exactly does it say that in the constitution?

Rogue Writer: Well I believe that somewhere in the boilerplate it says something like, "All men are created equal."

Donald Dump: Yeah and that was written by a bunch of privileged land owners and slave owners. I guess that tells you how sincere they were. They were pols just like the modern day pols. They said one thing but really meant another. I mean like do you mean to tell me that the Donald was created equal to everyone else. I don't think so.

Rogue Writer: Are all pols dishonest?

Donald Dump: Of course they are. Come out from your cave. That's why pols spend all that money on political advertising - trying to convince the voters they're honest. That's half the battle in politics - making people think you're honest - when you're not.

Rogue Writer: What's the other half then?

Donald Dump: Enacting policy that makes it legal to steal from the little people.

Rogue Writer: And how do you do that?

Donald Dump: Hire good lawyers. That's what good lawyers do - steal from the other guys. That's what my book: *The Art of the Steal* is all about. Did you read it?

Rogue Writer: I got about three pages into it and started to vomit.

Donald Dump: Good sense of humor. I like that. Listen, Joe six pack understands me because I tell it like it is. People don't understand all the complex policy stuff that the Bernie Sanders of the world are trying to peddle ... and by the way, Bernie spends half of his time out there shaking money tree. The only difference between him and me is that he's taking money from the little guys and I take my money from people who can afford to give it.

Rogue Writer: Rich people like yourself.

Donald Dump: Exactly, and that way we can insure that the system is wired to our own advantage.

Rogue Writer: Shifting gears here, you haven't said much in this campaign about the environment. What's you assessment about the current state of the earth's ecosystem?

Donald Dump: What kind of a bullshit question is that?

Rogue Writer: It's a good one. It affects every one of us as well as future generations.

Donald Dump: Listen if you're some greenie commando we can stop this interview right now. I have had it up to here with some holier than thou eco-kamikaze who places the welfare of the Salt Marsh Harvest Mouse of the Clinker Rail above the welfare of thousands of jobs and the march of progress.

Rogue Writer: So would it be safe to say you're not going to be courting the green vote?

Donald Dump: I'm sticking with my base and they don't give a shit about all this climate change double talk. People care about their pocketbooks not some distant danger that may or may not be real - and certainly won't affect anybody for at least fifty years.

Rogue Writer: What about after 50 years?

Donald Dump: We'll all be six feet under by then - and our remains will be helping to replenish the soils.

Rogue Writer: I don't get why you don't actually respond to people who ask you to explain how exactly you plan to round up 11 million undocumented immigrants and haul them off in boxcars. And what about the 14th amendment?

Donald Dump: Where do I start to show you where you're wrong. I've got some very good lawyers - some of the best in the business - and for much less that they'd charge anybody else they tell me that there are good reasons why the 14th amendment is wrong.

Rogue Writer: The 14th amendment is wrong?

Donald Dump: … Exactly … you're learning kid. Keep it up and I might hire you, to carry my bags.

Rogue Writer: Carry the bag of a rogue Presidential Candidate like you?

Donald Dump: Kid … you just nailed it. That's me I'm a rogue - a scoundrel. In politics and business we're all scoundrels. We're always selling somebody a dream. We're all looking for that secret sauce … that way of getting inside peoples brains and controlling their brains. Fortunately most people have been programmed to value money … money … above all else. And that's how I get inside their brains. Money is the vortex that leads inside people's brains. And sooner or later everyone alive gets sucking or seduced into that vortex.

Rogue Writer: So your whole Presidential campaign is a sham?

Donald Dump: Exactly,. All Presidential campaigns are a sham to some degree. That's what politicians do. We dangle promises and dreams of riches before the voters eyes.

Rogue Writer: And the dreams you're dangling are?

Donald Dump: I say everything I do as President will be terrific. They don't want to know more than that - because the rich people who own the media outlets have sedated all these people. Each night when they turn on the evening news on the boob tube … or every time they check their screens we're numbing their brains.

Rogue Writer: Is it working for America though. What's this turning America into?

Donald Dump: It's turning America into a bunch of zombies. That's what I mean when I say I'll "Make America Great Again." I'll snap the Zombies out of their zone, because I'm tearing up the old playbook of politics. I'm taking on the networks - penetrating

If Donald Trump becomes president.

the veneer of the seasoned pols - just by telling the truth about how bad things have become.

Rogue Writer: Is this progress?

Donald Dump: Who cares if it's progress. All I care about is that they they eat it up. People don't think for themselves any more. They too tired, mentally. So they don't question some scoundrel like me who's telling them everything is going to be terrific if you just vote for the Donald. Yes ..... I'm a rogue candidate ... Yes I'm a walking ego. Yes, I'm a scoundrel. But the only thing that differentiates me from all the other scoundrels is that I admit it.

Looking for a Few Good People

We're on a mission of sorts. We're looking for reasonable people … honest people … clear thinking people … people who are mystified by the Donald Trump phenomenon … … people who bring some measure of perspective to the world … people who've had enough of people who've had enough … people who like to think and talk about actual solutions … people who've developed a resistance to people who say their terrific … people who have their ego in check …. people who actually have a life … people who are mildly terrified that someone with as many personality defects as Donald Trump has gotten this far in the campaign.

So there it is … to sum … we're looking for a few good people … no, we're looking for many good people - millions of people who are willing to call for a halt to this nonsense - people who are willing to do their part, however small to help Donald Trump de-activate himself.

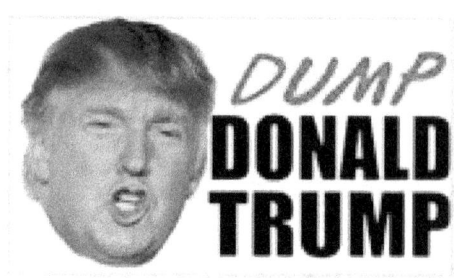

To become an official member of DTDS, you need only do three things.

1. Wake up.

2. Give reality a fighting chance. (All we are saying is give reality a chance.)

3. Sign the 3D (Donald Dump De-Activation) Petition - Please visit www.Donald-Dump.com.

The 3D Petition

(Donald Dump De-Activation)

Dear Donald:

Enough is enough. We've seen enough of this circus. Your carnival barker act is getting old. You're dragging down the debate. Your insults are insulting our intelligence. Stop this madness and stop it now. You are not a serious political candidate. Your ego is out of control. You are not adding anything of value to the political dialogue. You're an entertainer and this country needs someone who will offer serious solutions to serious problems. Get out of this race while the getting is good. For the sake of America's reputation on the world stage please take a hasty exit from politics. Be gone with you. De-activate yourself before the political process de-activates you.

Donald, you're fired.

Very Truly Yours,

Your name here

Appendix 1

Who Are These
Crazies?

Actual statements from Donald Trump's Supporters

A mystery has been perplexing all reasonable people - ever since Donald Trump declared for President and shot up to the top of the polls. Everyone can understand why the Donald is running - that's easy - to increase the value of the Donald Trump brand and to massage his own ego. But what we don't understand is the mentality of the people who are supporting him.

The whole thing blows our collective mind. Trump is a guy who owns real estate and charges people rents that are high enough to make him wads of money. Don't people realize that Trump is one of the class of rich bastards who are ripping them off? Plenty of pundits have been taking potshots at the Donald, but they're aiming at the wrong target. They're ignoring the people who are supporting the Donald. It's his supporters than give him credibility in the polls. Who are they? Where do they come from? What do they think, if anything? What do they feel? And what do they see in the Donald? That's the void I'm attempting to fill. Pay close attention to the astounding level of oversimplification and the gaping holes in logic.

Who Are These Crazies?

Love me some ...
... Trump.

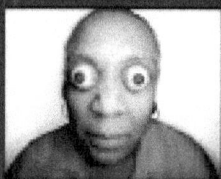

Kara Romano, 36
Gluing Machine Operator,
Peculiar, Missouri

Who Are These Crazies?

Yes! Be gone with these f**king aliens. I've
had it with them - stealing our jobs and
eating up all our food stamps.
Good for nothing f**kers.
I can't wait till the wall keeps them out.

Brant Guard, 72
Retired Forging Machine Operator,
Gripe, Arizona

Who Are These Crazies?

The Donald is The Man!!!

David Galvan, 42
Fundraiser,
Best, Texas

Who Are These Crazies?

Trump is the lead clown in the circus? Ha Ha Ha ... That is so not funny!

Annie Rook, 36
Foreign Language Teacher,
Baltimore, Maryland

Who Are These Crazies?

Politicians are boring.
The Donald isn't.

Teresa Booker, 36
Animal Breeder,
Cedar Rapids, Iowa

Who Are These Crazies?

We're mortgaging our future to the Chinese.
We don't manufacture anything any more.
The deficits are exploding. We need
somebody who will do something about
this. The Donald knows how to fix things.
He's a businessman.

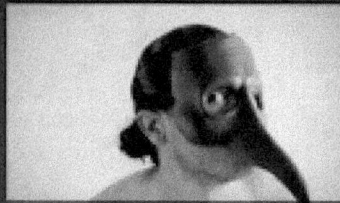

Reggie Rosha, 37
Electronic Drafter,
Two Egg, Florida

Who Are These Crazies?

Trump is getting my Hispanice vote ...

Rosalie Rosaly, 39
Farm Hand,
Mexican Water, Arizona

Who Are These Crazies?

He's a good man. You can't keep a good man down.

Chris Pinc, 27
Excavating Supervisor,
Pie Town, New Mexico

Who Are These Crazies?

Yup. I don't trust these demarats who hack the voting machines. They've probably decided the next three presidents.

Greg Garcia, 29
Furniture Finisher,
Success, Missouri

Who Are These Crazies?

What a wise man.
I almost shook his hand.

Ruthie Nicols, 44
Family Caseworker,
Birds Eye, Indiana

Who Are These Crazies?

I'm tired of the nation getting ripped off. I'm voting for the Donald.

Julian Jourard, 36
Gynecologist
Happyland, Connecticut

Who Are These Crazies?

Mr. Trump has neatly smacked the media into line, and cleverly routed his rivals.

Mike McHugh, 36
Fire Investigator
Buttermilk, Kansas

Who Are These Crazies?

The Donald has exposed the establishment. It's a sham!!!!

Teresa Booker, 36
Animal Breeder,
Cedar Rapids, Iowa

Donald Dump • The Ego Runs Wild • www.Donald-Dump.com   19

Who Are These Crazies?

He's so smart and I love his hair!

Teresa Booker, 36
Animal Breeder,
Cedar Rapids, Iowa

Donald Dump • The Ego Runs Wild • www.Donald-Dump.com   20

Who Are These Crazies?

He's been prescient on many issues.
It's like he has his own
crystal ball.

Bryce Jordan, 42
Survey Technician,
Bacon, Indiana

Who Are These Crazies?

I hope he wins, but I have a
funny feeling he's gonna get
screwed over by the
hidden establishment.

Aaron Ganz, 47
Health Psychologist,
Why, Arizona

Who Are These Crazies?

I'm worried about voter fraud, and high turnout of those on welfare who don't want to work. The "silent majority" must turn out in high numbers, if we want to get it done.

Sal Garbi, 36
Fashion Designer,
New York City, New York

Who Are These Crazies?

We're wasting billions on toilet seats for the military. Half of our country is on the dole. We've become a country of whiners and complainers. That's why I'm supporting Donald Trump. He doesn't whine. He just wins instead.

Mylos Petrini, 38
Set Illustrator,
Hippo, Kentucky

Who Are These Crazies?

Trump says it like it is, and that is being a REAL person. You may not always like the truth but someone has to say it and Trump is saying it well.

Everett Peyer, 67
Horticulture Therapist
Brainy Borough, New Jersey

Who Are These Crazies?

Hey, Trump's making sense. I'm all in for Trump. Any American that votes for Bush or Hillary, should be on the other side of Trump's wall.

Paul Petaway, 47
Hydraulic Engineer
Trout, Lousiana

Who Are These Crazies?

If Mr. Trump accepts my challenge to a fist fight and wins, I'll vote for him.

_____

Larry Evemeyer, 28
Title Searcher,
Cincinnati, Ohio

Who Are These Crazies?

Trump is **our** leader now!

_____

Teresa Endersby, 36
Travel Counselor,
Elk Grove, California

Who Are These Crazies?

Trump is a clown? Okay, but he's
$7 billion clown. He can buy and
sell you all day long.....can't he???

Chris Emery, 47
Travel Writer,
Greenwich, Connecticut

Who Are These Crazies?

The establishment is so scared of trump and
things being fixed. So many companies have
their hands in the government's wallet and
then give money to these politicians to keep
it all flowing. Trump will stop this!

Joseph Fahey, 68
Treatment Plant Operator,
Durham, New Hampshire

Who Are These Crazies?

9 clowns and one real man -
that should be the name of
these debates.

Jerry Bragstad, 36
Veterinary Assistant
Los Angeles, California

Who Are These Crazies?

EVERYONE PLEASE LISTEN ! IF WE DON'T ELECT TRUMP USA IS OVER WE
ARE AT 19 TRILLION THAT'S A "T" / 24 TRILLION IS THE MAGIC NUMBER
AND WE CAN BE LIKE GREECE AND OUR DOLLARS CAN BE WIPE AS
NAPKINS, BY THE TIME OBAMA LEAVES IT WILL BE 21 TRILLION THINK OF
THIS WE NEED A BUSINESS MAN TO PUT OUR COUNTRY BACK ON THE
RIGHT PATH "REMEMBER POLITICIAN ALL TALK NO ACTION / SUCKING
THE BLOOD OUT OF US" IT'S TOTALLY ENOUGH THE KEY TO THIS
COUNTRY & REGAIN ITS GROUND IS TO TREAT AND HELP HEAL ITS
WOUND TRUMP2016 ALLLLTHEWAYYYY

Arthur Brendze, 36
Insurance Claims Adjuster,
Denver, Colorado

Who Are These Crazies?

You been watching bad medias and press about Trump and got brainwashed by these idiots ... come on be smarter!!!!!

Richard Janiker, 43
Dentist,
Oatmeal, Texas

Who Are These Crazies?

ALL THESE POLITICIANS ARE CORRUPT AS FUCK IF THEY CAN LISTEN TO THAT AND COMPLETELY IGNORE THE IDEA OF FIXING THE LAWS THAT PROMOTE THE RICH 1% ...

Earl Flint, 42
Sewer Inspector
Lodi, California

Who Are These Crazies?

I am voting for Trump at least he is honest about what is going on here.

Rick Flaster, 43
Insurance Estate Planner,
Provo, Utah

Who Are These Crazies?

Trump isn't lying about the idiots who are running this country into the ground.

David Gardella, 46
Food and Drug Inspector,
Ham Lake, Minnesota

Who Are These Crazies?

He radiates confidence and
that's what makes a man
in this world.

Jony McCure, 52
Fraud Investigator,
Lick Fork, Virginia

Who Are These Crazies?

He's closing statement with the
example on how he negotiated
the time down to 2 hrs
was a grand slam.

Andrew Finnegan, 36
Waiter
San Francisco, California

Who Are These Crazies?

Trump has so much energy!

Lynda Fiesel, 36
Watch Repairer,
Tuscaloosa, Alabama

Who Are These Crazies?

Trump, wants to get rid of superpacks
that ruin the country.
To me that makes him sound like the only
person who cares a tiny bit.

Paul Fillow, 26
Storage Manager,
Savannah, Georgia

Who Are These Crazies?

This guy is a rock star of personality like politics has never seen.

Tim Flinders, 36
Telecommunications Line Installers,
Pittsburgh, Pennsylvania

Who Are These Crazies?

The fact that everything he touches turns to gold for him proves he lives up to his persona. Trump 2016!!!!!

Mary Finali, 76
Grandmother of 46
St Louis, Missouri

Appendix 2

ATDA

Ask the Donald Anything

Donald, where do you get your arm candy?

- Scotty Baublez, 43
Private Equity Partner
New York City, NY

Donald Dump - As you know, Scotty, having the right arm candy is critical to a your credibility and, by the way, all my wives have been gorgeous. Fortunately, beautiful women are attracted to me so I don't have to get them - they fight to get me.

Donald Dump • The Ego Runs Wild • www.Donald-Dump.com   1

Ask The Donald Anything

How did it feel to be roasted by the President at the White House correspondent's dinner?

- Jay Gatsby, 53
Businessman
West Egg, New York

Donald Dump: It wasn't funny. He got a few cheap laughs at my expense. Can you imagine me ever insulting people like that? I'm too dignified to stoop that low.

Donald Dump • The Ego Runs Wild • www.Donald-Dump.com   2

Ask The Donald Anything

What are you doing
next Saturday night?

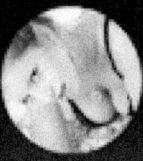

- Joy Booker -
Art Therapist
Beaver Lick, OK

Donald Dump - I like
your credentials. I'll be
in touch ... so to speak.

Donald Dump • The Ego Runs Wild • www.Donald-Dump.com   3

Ask The Donald Anything

Who's your favorite
comic book character?

- Susan Huller - 8
Child Actress
Culver City, CA

Donald Dump:
Superman ... The
similarities are almost
eerie - see for yourself.

Donald Dump • The Ego Runs Wild • www.Donald-Dump.com   4

Ask The Donald Anything

Why do you scrape the toppings off a pizza and never eat the crust?

- Charles Home - 61 -
Hedge Fund Manager - La Jolla, CA

Donald Dump - To keep my weight down. It's also the way I approach life in general. I take the toppings of what life has to offer. Other people stuff themselves on the carbs and just get fat. Take Rosie O'Donnell for example. Please - take her!

Donald Dump • The Ego Runs Wild • www.Donald-Dump.com   5

Ask The Donald Anything

If you had you're life to live over again what would you change?

- Ben Hovermail - 57 - Funeral
Director - Bitter Springs, AZ

Donald Dump - Nothing ...
... next question.

Donald Dump • The Ego Runs Wild • www.Donald-Dump.com   6

Ask The Donald Anything

As President what are you going to do for rich people like us?

- General Partners
Lumpkin, Pumkpin and Cool,
Greenwich, CT

Donald Dump - We need to talk privately about this. I can tell you, off the record, that it's going to be terrific - really terrific - to be rich when I'm President.

Ask The Donald Anything

How stupid do you think we are?

- Sofia Kadin, 28 -
Aquarium Curator
Chevy Chase, MD

Donald Dump: A lot more stupid that you realize you are.

Ask The Donald Anything

How did you calculate the $3 billion figure for the value of your personal brand?

- Jess Normandy, 34 -
Private Investor
Gross Point Farms, MI

Donald Dump - I took one billion and multiplied it by three. By the way, that value has increased by at least 50% since I announced for President. Win or lose the nomination, I win.

Donald Dump • The Ego Runs Wild • www.Donald-Dump.com   9

Ask The Donald Anything

Do you have any actual policy proposals?

- Gene Kornfeld, 38
Mapping Technician,
Coinjock, NC

Donald Dump - If I did I wouldn't share them publicly. Voters don't care about that stuff. They want excitement ... they want fireworks ... not a whole lot of excitement in the small details of policy. But lots of fireworks in personal attacks.

Donald Dump • The Ego Runs Wild • www.Donald-Dump.com   10

Ask The Donald Anything

What with you're testy relationship with the media?

- Alan Thelin and Friends
Real Estate Sales
Brentwood, CA

Donald Dump - I have a great relationship with the media. Reporters love me because I give them something new and different to write about. Most of these guys are jaded. They eat up what I say because it's bold, it's provocative and it's usually true. I've broken all the old rules of campaigning ... and the other guys are jealous - they're trying to imitate me but nobody can imitate the Donald.

Donald Dump • The Ego Runs Wild • www.Donald-Dump.com   11

Ask The Donald Anything

What historical figures do you look up to?

- Levester Kilgore - 35
Talent Agent
Los Angeles, CA

Donald Dump - Lev ...
you got it backwards ...
... they look up to me.

Donald Dump • The Ego Runs Wild • www.Donald-Dump.com   12

Ask The Donald Anything

Donald, what **really** motivates you?

- Edwin Judd - 41
Money Manager
Los Angeles, CA

Donald Dump - Same thing that motivate you and everyone else in our circles ... Ed.

Ask The Donald Anything

What's with you and Megan Kelly?

- Teresa Hooker, 29
Goodside and Broadview
Miami, FL

Donald Dump - Fox doesn't hire people for their reporting skills or intelligence. They hire them for their looks. Megan, is ... well ... you saw her.

Ask The Donald Anything

Who's your favorite author?

- Flo Booker 37
Librarian, Wise, VA

Donald Dump - Generally, I don't read books. Instead, I read executive summaries. The only books I've ever read were written by the Donald.

Ask The Donald Anything

Who does your hair?

- Margo Segal, 28
- Model, New York City, NY

Donald Dump - We do it in house with a full time staff of four. Then we have another eight consultants that we bring in on an as needed basis. You never know when you're going to have a bad hair day.

Ask The Donald Anything

How many homes do **you** have? I''ve got eight.

- Larry Terzian, 47
Various Occupations
Various Locations

Donald Dump - I'm not sure exactly, but it's at least a hundred - maybe a thousand. By the way, I don't live in them all, but it's comforting to know that they're there ... if need them.

Donald Dump • The Ego Runs Wild • www.Donald-Dump.com   17

Ask The Donald Anything

What makes you think you can cut taxes by $10 trillion and still balance the budget?

- Jon Tibbits, 63
Dermatologist, Bethesda, MD

Donald Dump - I've had 4 bankruptcies and each time I came out smelling like a rose. American has $19 trillion in debt. I know how to handle debt. If you want someone who can manage the budget then put me in the White House.

Donald Dump • The Ego Runs Wild • www.Donald-Dump.com   18

Ask The Donald Anything

Can someone be tell the truth
and still succeed in politics today?

- Analyst Pay 34
Inspector, Egg Harbor, NJ

_____

Donald Dump - Honestly - yes you can. You just
have to know when to tell the truth and when to
lie. That's what separates me from all the other
career pols in Washington. I know when and how to
lie to my own advantage better than all the other
chronic liars in government.

Donald Dump • The Ego Runs Wild • www.Donald-Dump.com   19

Ask The Donald Anything

My favorite color is red. What's yours?

- Jud Keene, 45
Venture Capitalist
San Francisco, CA

_____

Donald Dump - Depends on where
I'm flying in my private jet. My favorite
color is the color of money. In some
countries it's green. In others it's red.

Donald Dump • The Ego Runs Wild • www.Donald-Dump.com   20

Ask The Donald Anything

What makes the Donald
Trump brand so
valuable?

- Frank Tessin, 43
Comptroller,
Cologne, MN

Donald Dump - It's valuable because,
I say it's valuable.   People believe
anything I say - because I'm the Donald.

Ask The Donald Anything

What one piece of advice do
you have for all the little
people out there?

- Sean Rozelle, 54
Consultant - San Francisco, CA

Donald Dump - The best
advice I can give is very simply –
let your ego run wild and free.

Ask The Donald Anything

What's it like being rich?

- Robert Pawlow
Homeless. - Chicago, IL

Donald Dump - I love being rich. Being rich is terrific. I wish everyone could be as terrific as I am. You should try being rich ... you'll love it.

Donald Dump • The Ego Runs Wild • www.Donald-Dump.com   23

Ask The Donald Anything

I understand you're a teetotaler. Why don't you drink?

- Frederick Timms -
Waiter
Ames, Iowa

Donald Dump - Alcohol makes you stupid ... I'm too smart to be stupid.

Donald Dump • The Ego Runs Wild • www.Donald-Dump.com   24

Ask The Donald Anything

How can I be rich like you?

- David Seegar, 34
Plant Breedeer- Bug Tussle, OK

Donald Dump - You just have to keep planting seeds. Talk to me later. I'm sure we can cut a deal.

Ask The Donald Anything

What kind of a man are you, really?

- Ether Seiderman, 32
Supermodel - Miami, FL

Donald Dump - I'm more than a man. I'm a movement – "The Donald Movement." By the way, I'm much more virile and potent than any other candidate I've got the hair to prove it.

Ask The Donald Anything

What makes you different
from all the other
phony pols?

- Brian Sharkey 35
Investment Advisor
Westhampton, NY

Donald Dump - I'm not a pol. I don't think
like a pol. I'm a no nonsense guy. I'm tough.
I'm smart and I'm a great negotiator. Just ask
my lawyers, my bankers and my ex-wives.

Donald Dump • The Ego Runs Wild • www.Donald-Dump.com   27

Ask The Donald Anything

How do you expect to win the
Latino vote when you're
consistently racist?

- Carlos Lopez, 28
Order Clerk, Phoenix, AZ

Donald Dump - Latino's love
me. I've hired tons of them to
clean my mansions and castles.

Donald Dump • The Ego Runs Wild • www.Donald-Dump.com   28

Ask The Donald Anything

How can you be both a
populist and part
of the 1%?

- Ethan Rockal, 34
Philosopher, Philadelphia, PA

Donald Dump - It's easy. I just attack the establishment and soon people forget that I'm part of the establishment. Everybody hates the establishment. I hate the establishment. So we're all united by our hate of the establishment. I'm rich, ... so what ... I'm an independent, populist rich guy.

Donald Dump • The Ego Runs Wild • www.Donald-Dump.com   29

Ask The Donald Anything

What's your campaign all
about - really Donald?

- Pat McHill, 37
Banker, Perfection, NY

Donald Dump - It's real simple - a vote for the Donald is a vote to increase the value of the Donald's brand.

Donald Dump • The Ego Runs Wild • www.Donald-Dump.com   30

Ask The Donald Anything

How will you break the stalemate in Congress?

- Liza Payne 29,
Collector - Grand Rapids, MI

Donald Dump - Washington is a mess today. It's a disaster. They can't balance the budget. They spend more than they have to the tune of $19 trillion in debt. When I'm elected I'll call a spade a spade and I'll declare Washington a disaster zone - and we'll allocate sufficient funds to clean it up.

Donald Dump • The Ego Runs Wild • www.Donald-Dump.com   31

Ask The Donald Anything

What are the secrets to your success?

- Vincent Sabis
Tax Lawyer - Scrabble, VA

Donald Dump - I owe my success to my good looks, my magnetic personality, my positive attitude, my amazing intelligence and - most of all - I'd like to thank my wonderful alter ego – **The Donald.**

Donald Dump • The Ego Runs Wild • www.Donald-Dump.com   32

Ask The Donald Anything

How do you maintain your
credibility while breaking
your promises?

- Cathleen Richardson 38
Funraiser, Deep Tunnel, NH

Donald Dump - You have to do it selectively.
The pols in Washington are always making
promises they can't keep. They do it so much they
don't even realize they're doing it.   But when I
make a promise I can't keep I know what I'm doing.

Donald Dump • The Ego Runs Wild • www.Donald-Dump.com   33

Ask The Donald Anything

How important is having
a big ego to being a
success in today's world?

- Al Steigler, 39
Furniture Designer
- Dry Fork, VA

Donald   Dump - Absolutely
essential. Having a big ego is what
made the Donald the sucess he is.

Donald Dump • The Ego Runs Wild • www.Donald-Dump.com   34

Ask The Donald Anything

What's the secret to being a good negotiator?

- Pat Saige, 46
Tax Collector, Needmore, PA

Donald Dump - The secret to being a good negotiator is to have more leverage ie. money, than the other guy. That's why I'm such a great negotiator.

Ask The Donald Anything

What percentage of your life do you spend stroking your own ego?

- Claire North 33
Nurse, Overlook, AL

Donald Dump - At least 60% - on my good days it's over 90%.

Ask The Donald Anything

How many wives should a "successful" man have had in his life?

- James. J. Rothmuller, 26
Limousine Driver
Darien, CT

Donald Dump - Three is the absolute minimum. You need them to prove that you're a real man. I'd suggest more depending on your potency.

Donald Dump • The Ego Runs Wild • www.Donald-Dump.com   37

Ask The Donald Anything

What's your solution to the national debt?

William Rotz, 37
Budget Analyst
- Palm Beach, FL

Donald Dump - America is a huge debtor nation. I'm an expert on debt. I know how to handle too much debt and that's what America needs today - someone who knows how to "manage" his way out of too much debt.

Donald Dump • The Ego Runs Wild • www.Donald-Dump.com   38

Ask The Donald Anything

How much money is too much money?

- Samuel Sadin, 46
Financial Services Sales Agent
Idiot Creek, Oregon

Donald Dump - You can never have too much money. A man needs money to prove he's successful. Have you ever heard of someone who was too successful. Never ...

Ask The Donald Anything

What's the number one reason I should vote for the Donald?

'OH MY GOD, IT'S SO HUGE!'

- Jennifer Weiner
Structural Engineer, Climax, AL

Donald Dump - The answer may surprise you, Jen. Remember I owned the Miss America Beauty Pageant. I know about beauty. I'm an expert on beauty. If you want to be looking at something nice - something really nice - for the next four years, vote for the Donald.

Ask The Donald Anything

What's your position on taxes?

- Lisa Sapuppo, 37
Tourguide, Bat Cave, NC

Donald Dump - Everybody - and I mean everybody - pays too much in taxes today. Elect me and everybody will pay less - it's that simple. And by the way I'll also balance the budget by raising taxes on everyone else.

Donald Dump • The Ego Runs Wild • www.Donald-Dump.com   41

Ask The Donald Anything

What's with these pols who talk out of both sides of their mouth?

- Donald Rheingold 56
Speech Pathologist
Defiance, NM

Donald Dump - Hey, I'm a businessman. I'm not a politician. I tell it like it is. I don't sugar coat things. I know how to get things done because I'm an outsider. And I know the right people and together we'll turn the outsiders into insiders.

Donald Dump • The Ego Runs Wild • www.Donald-Dump.com   42

Ask The Donald Anything

What's your secret to deceiving people?

- Claire Perkins, 45
Psychologist, Boston, MA

Donald Dump - I've been deceiving people for so long, I don't think about it any more. At first it felt strange, but it just feels natural to deceive people now. That's what I do. It's what made the Donald who he is – deception.

Ask The Donald Anything

So you're a businessman, but how does that make you qualified to run the government?

- Tomas Koon, 69
Shipping Magnate
Sag Harbor, NY

Donald Dump - Listen, I understand business. That's why I'm now worth between $5 and $10 billion depending on which set of numbers I use. In government, as in business, you have to be able to use numbers creatively – to your own advantage.

Ask The Donald Anything

What do you think of Citizens United?

- Geraldine Pearlman, 75
Heiress, New York City, NY

Donald Dump - It was a very poor decision. It opened up the floodgates for rich people to take over Washington. Because I'm self financing my campaign, I'm not beholden to other rich people. I'm only answerable to one rich person - the Donald.

Donald Dump • The Ego Runs Wild • www.Donald-Dump.com   45

Ask The Donald Anything

What's wit the all da dudes that ain't got no cludes?

- Charles Jone, 32
Rapper
Badass, New Jersey

Donald Dump - Washington is a madhouse these days. They're clueless. The loonies are running the show. When I'm elected we'll get all the crazies out of Washington. We'll replace the old loonies with a new set of loonies.

Donald Dump • The Ego Runs Wild • www.Donald-Dump.com   46

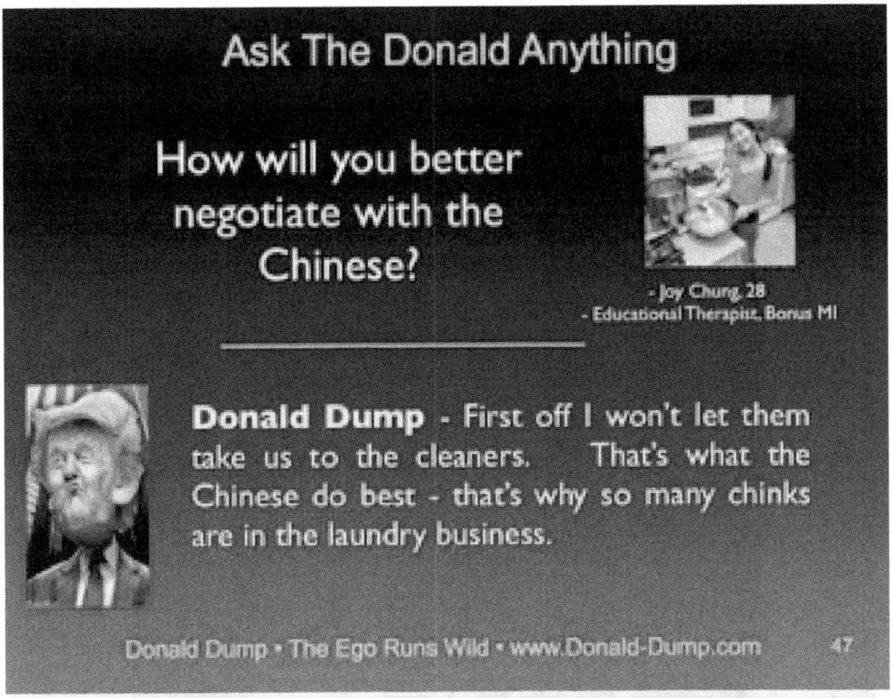

Ask The Donald Anything
How will you better negotiate with the Chinese?
- Joy Chung, 28
- Educational Therapist, Bonus MI
Donald Dump - First off I won't let them take us to the cleaners. That's what the Chinese do best - that's why so many chinks are in the laundry business.
Donald Dump • The Ego Runs Wild • www.Donald-Dump.com
47

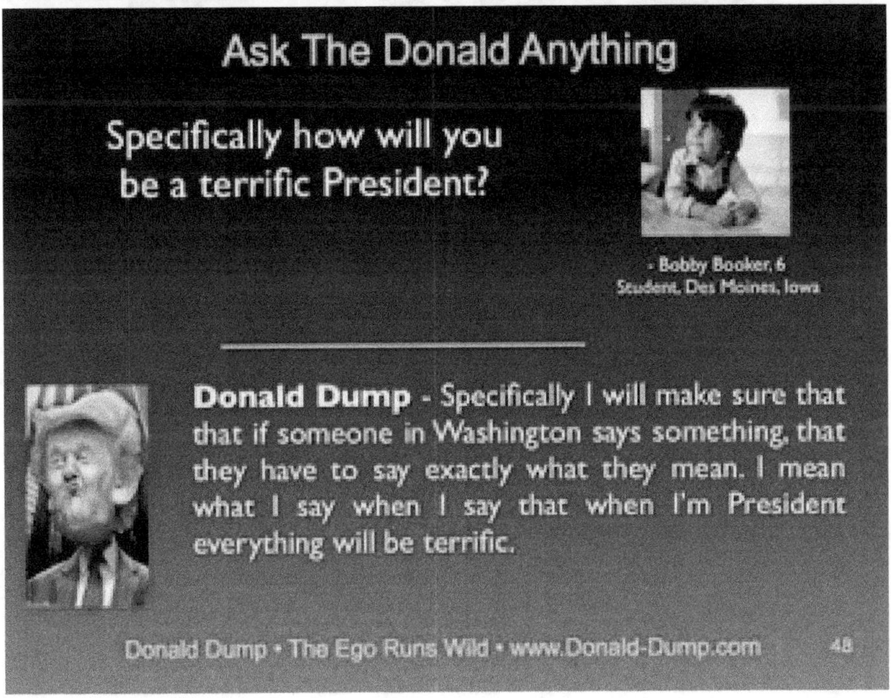

Ask The Donald Anything
Specifically how will you be a terrific President?
- Bobby Booker, 6
Student, Des Moines, Iowa
Donald Dump - Specifically I will make sure that that if someone in Washington says something, that they have to say exactly what they mean. I mean what I say when I say that when I'm President everything will be terrific.
Donald Dump • The Ego Runs Wild • www.Donald-Dump.com
48

Appendix 3

Imagine all the knowledge sits just below
The Donald's a big quaff of hair.

DDT

Donald Dump
Translates

A More Noxious and Toxic Form of DDT

According to Wikipedia - *DDT (dichlorodiphenyltrichloroethane) is a colorless, crystalline, tasteless and almost odorless organochloride known for its insecticidal properties. ... In 1962, the book Silent Spring by American biologist Rachel Carson was published. It cataloged the environmental impacts of indiscriminate DDT spraying in the United States and questioned the logic of releasing large amounts of potentially dangerous chemicals into the environment without a sufficient understanding of their effects on ecology or human health.*

Now history has introduce a new DDT - every bit as toxic as the old DDT - colorless, odorless chemical form but more pervasive - more noxious and more dangerous than the old DDT. Until Rachel Carson who wrote Silent Spring and people didn't know about DDT and what it's deleterious effects were.

In a very real sense we're looking at a Silent Spring if Donald Trump gets the nomination in Spring of 2016 or otherwise is around to exert leverage on the outcome of the campaign. It will be silent because people's minds will have been numbed by the new strains of DDT coming out of Donald Trumps mouth. They will be mesmerized by the uncanny way every thought and every question somehow ends up in puffery - the kind of puffery - mystifying combination of artfully condensing words that sends out a smokescreen to obscure all the contradictions that lie inside the ego-driven man who has captured the attention of America. The DDT coming out from Donald Dumps mouth deflects the internal inconsistencies of his head fakes, for millions of unsuspecting viewers.

To be or not to be...
That is the question.
- **William Shakespeare**

DDT - Donald Dump Translates:

Cut the crap!
Let's get down to business.

Donald Dump • The Ego Runs Wild • www.Donald-Dump.com   1

I think ...
Therefore I am.
- **René Descartes**

DDT - Donald Dump Translates:

I think I'm the Donald ...

Therefore, I am the Donald!

Donald Dump • The Ego Runs Wild • www.Donald-Dump.com   2

Move confidently in the
direction of your dreams.
Live the life you have imagined.

- Henry David Thoreau

DDT - Donald Dump Translates:

You can't imagine me being President?
What's your problem?

Donald Dump • The Ego Runs Wild • www.Donald-Dump.com   3

I don't make commitments
and then break them.
- **Donald Trump**

DDT - Donald Dump Translates:

It was only four bankruptcies?
Everybody does it.
It's part of being a good businessman.

Donald Dump • The Ego Runs Wild • www.Donald-Dump.com   4

Politics is the art of the possible, the attainable - the art of the next best.
- **Otto Von Bismark**

DDT - Donald Dump Translates:

Hey, politics is simple.
It's like business – build your brand.
Then promote the hell out of it.

Donald Dump • The Ego Runs Wild • www.Donald-Dump.com   5

Most folks are as happy as they make up their minds to be.
- **Abraham Lincoln**

DDT - Donald Dump Translates:

Hey, I'm a happy guy. Why?
Because I made up my mind to be terrific.
If you're terrific, you're happy.

Donald Dump • The Ego Runs Wild • www.Donald-Dump.com   6

I want to know God's thoughts
... the rest are details.
- **Albert Einstein**

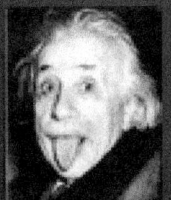

DDT - Donald Dump Translates:

I like God. I think God has done a lot of good
for a lot of people. He deserves all the credit
he gets in churches. But, God is not anywhere
near the force I am in the world today.

Donald Dump • The Ego Runs Wild • www.Donald-Dump.com   7

100% of the shots you
don't take don't go in.
- **Wayne Gretzky**

DDT - Donald Dump Translates:

100% of my shots go in.
Hey, I'm the Donald ...

... I'm a big shot.

Donald Dump • The Ego Runs Wild • www.Donald-Dump.com   8

Would you tell me, please, which way
I ought to go from here?'
'That depends a good deal on where you
want to get to,' said the Cat.
'I don't much care where --' said Alice.

Donald Dump Translates:

I know exactly where I'm going ...
... straight to the White House!

An eye for eye only ends
up making the whole world blind.
- M.K. Gandhi

DDT - Donald Dump Translates:

I look the other guy right in the eye.
I want to know who's blind and
who see things my way.

Shakespeare on The Donald

To-morrow, and to-morrow, and to-morrow,
Creeps in this petty pace from day to day,
To the last syllable of recorded time;
And all our yesterdays have lighted fools
The way to dusty death.
Out, out, brief candle!
Life's but a walking shadow, a poor player,
That struts and frets his hour upon the stage,
And then is heard no more. It is a tale
Told by an idiot, full of sound and fury,
Signifying nothing.

Macbeth, Act 5, Scene Five

Other Amazing Books by John F. Ince
All Available on Amazon ...

Travels With Vanessa

Book 1 - A Rideshare Driver
Tries To Make Sense of It All

By John F. Ince
aka The Rogue Writer

Repugnicance

The 2012 Version of the Republican Bible Babble

John F. Ince
AKA - George Won't
Columnist for the Washington Pissed

Repugnicants

The Wacky World of Republican Politics

Featuring:
Snoot Gingrich, Snit Romney, Run Paul,
P.Rick Perry, Michele Babblethump,
Herman Pizza and Donald Dump

John F. Ince
AKA - George Won't
Columnist for the *Washington Pissed*

Mitt Romney

The King of Bain

and the Man Who Wants To Be
The President

By John F. Ince

Snitt Romney

The Repugnicant Candidate
For President of the
Untied States of America

BY JOHN F. INCE

Sarah Palin

Going ~~Rogue~~
Rude

The Official Handbook of the
Sarah Palin Admiration Society

THE
WIZ OF IZ

A STORY ABOUT THE POWER OF INSPIRED LEADERSHIP, THE BIRTH OF A MOVEMENT AND THE TRIUMPH OF

HOPE

JOHN F. INCE

Meaningful
MONEY

INNOVATION AT THE
INTERSECTION OF ...

MONEY, MEANING
AND MARKETS

JOHN F. INCE

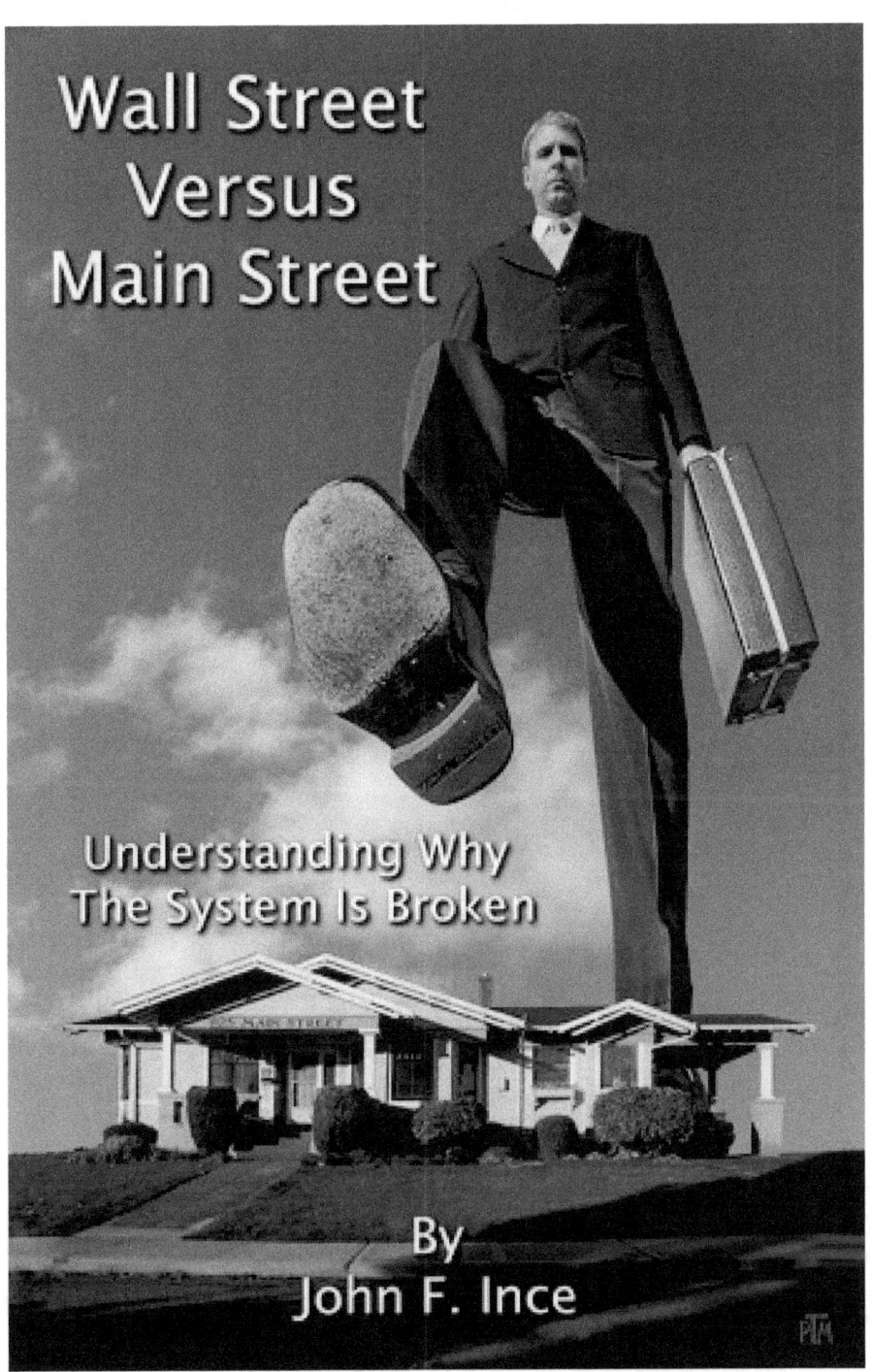

Wall Street
Versus
Main Street

Understanding Why
The System Is Broken

By
John F. Ince

Main Street
Versus
Wall Street

Transforming Raw Anger
Into Purposeful Action

John F. Ince

THE CODE OF
COMMON
CENTS

NEW MONEY VS OLD MONEY
AND THE NEXT
AMERICAN REVOLUTION

JOHN F. INCE

About the Author - John F. Ince
a. k. a. The *Rogue* Writer

The author of this body of work is much older and more stupider than he looks. In fact, he's 67 years old and his IQ is so low it doesn't even register on most thermometers. Although he has now written 15 books, he's still a bit of an odd duck when it comes to creative expression. None of his books fit into any established literary genre and they tend to defy both common sense and convention. For example, he does not, in general, agree with the whole notion of punctuation. But like his reluctant acceptance of using utensils at mealtime, he does find periods and commas occasionally useful.

None of his books have ever received much attention despite their amazing content and transcendent qualities. It's entirely his fault that they've never been widely promoted or sold. He's not good at self promotion - which is why his writing a book about a self-promotional master like Donald Trump is so ironic. If you have somehow discovered this book, be sure to keep it too yourself. We wouldn't want Ince's crazy ideas to get out and possibly infect mainstream literature.

Ince cut his teeth on the "trade" of journalism trade almost 40 years ago while a reporter for *Fortune Magazine*. Between then and now he's made gallant attempts to advance himself in such promising careers as - social enterprise, lawn maintenance, lacrosse refereeing, podcasting, Uber driving, Wall Street banking, resort development, environmental education, tech startups, nonprofit fundraising and documentary filmmaking. He's never made much money doing any of this, which is why he's still working feverishly. He has no idea where most of his ideas come from - other than occasional visitations from the muse at odd moments, often in the middle of the night or when he is going to the bathroom.

While Ince's outlook is decidedly unconventional, he dresses nicely – but not flamboyantly. Like clockwork, he does his laundry once a year on the second Tuesday of September, whether it needs it or not. He graduated from both Harvard College where he was an undergraduate housemate of Al Gore and Harvard Business School, in the same class of Mitt Romney. His political leanings are difficult to categorize. He has grave reservations about both Repugnicants and Democraps, but he usually votes for one or the other depending on how much he likes the sound of each candidate's name.